The POWER Series

US Air Force
SPECIAL OPS

Fred J. Pushies

MBI Publishing Company

Dedication
To the Air Commandos past, present, and future.

First published in 2000 by MBI Publishing Company, 729 Prospect Avenue, PO Box 1, Osceola, WI 54020-0001 USA

MBI Publishing Company books are also available at discounts in bulk quantity for industrial or sales-promotional use. For details write to Special Sales Manager at Motorbooks International Wholesalers & Distributors, 729 Prospect Avenue, PO Box 1, Osceola, WI 54020-0001 USA.

Library of Congress Cataloging-in-Publication Data
Pushies, Fred J.
  U.S. Air Force Special Ops / Fred J. Pushies.
    p.cm. -- (The power series)
  Includes index.
  ISBN 0-7603-0733-4 (pbk. : alk paper)
    1. United States. Air Force Special Operations Command--History. 2. Special forces (Military science)--United States--History. 3. United States. Air Force--Commando troops. I. Title: US Air Force Special Ops. II Title. III Power series (Osceola, Wis.)
UG633 .p87 2000
358.4--dc21

Front Cover: While a combat controller on SATCOM provides air traffic control of the airhead, a PJ on M-4 provides security and remains ready to provide emergency medical treatment as the mission progresses.

Frontispiece: The business end of the GAU-12/U 25-millimeter Gatling cannon on an AC-130U Spectre Gunship. The cannon is fully traversable and capable of firing 1,800 rounds per minute (thats 30 rounds each second) from altitudes of up to 12,000 feet.

Title Page: The mission of the MH-53J Pave Low III helicopter is to carry out low-level, long-range, undetected ingress into denied or hostile areas. This is accomplished day or night, even under the worst weather conditions for infiltration, exfiltration, and resupply of special operations forces.

Back Cover: For any special operation force operating in a forward area close to the enemy, concealment is key, and often necessary to have against a numerically superior opponent. All commandos are taught how to use cover to their advantage.

Edited by Michael Haenggi
Designed by Bruce Leckie

Printed in China

Table of Contents

First, I want to thank God that we live in a country where freedom and liberty are more than concepts: they are our way of life. A special thanks to the men and women of AFSOC who put it on the line daily to keep it that way. I thank the following individuals for their assistance in making this book possible: Michael Haenggi, editor, MBI Publishing; Sergeant Herman, U.S. Air Force recruiting; Lieutenant Colonel M. Durham; Captain G. Fischer; Senior Master Sergeant P. Rhodes; Shirley Pouge; Sandy Henry; Captain D. Berry, Air Force Special Operations Command, Public Affairs Office (AFSOC); Captain Charles Stoner and AC-130U crew 4th Special Operations Squadron (SOS); Lt. Colonel Tim Shaffer, 4th SOS; the Pave Low crews of the 20th SOS, the Green Hornets; Captain Tom Dermody, Captain Chris Lambert, Staff Sergeant Donny Wright, Technical Sergeant Eddie Linnbaum, Technical Sergeant Robert Smith, Senior Airman Brian McDaniel; Lt. Colonel Ken Rodriguez, Major Michael Sneeder; Staff Sergeant Bob Benton and team, the 23rd Special Tactics Squadron (STS); Staff Sergeant Terry Saltzman, Senior Airman John Chilcoat; Mr. Herb Mason; Charlie Jones, Chief Warrant Officer (ret.), Air Commando Association; Captain Kris Koller, 193rd SOS.; Mike McKinney, Knight Manufacturing Company; David Hale, Insight Technology Incorporated; Timothy M. Jensen, Rockwell; Mr. Ron Childress, Master Sergeant (ret.); the IFAM cadre: Technical Sergeant Bart Decker, Technical Sergeant Dirk Wenrich, and Staff Sergeant Rick Driggers; Crew of "Niner-One-Niner," MC-130 Papa Duke Air Force Base; Robert Genat; Lieutenant M. Chavis, 324 TRS; Monica Manganero, Fort Benning PAO; Carol Darby, USASOC PAO, Fort Bragg; Doug Kinneard, Boeing; Mr. Ola Bericksing, Borfors, Sweden; Master Sergeant Paul Venturella, Combat Control School, Pope Air Force Base; Irene Witt, 37th Training Wing PAO; Captain Barb Carson, Kirtland Air Force Base PAO; Master Sergeant David Lee and Master Sergeant Rick Weaver, Pararescue School, Kirtland Air Force Base; and Gene Adcock, Vice President Night Vision Equipment Company.

I also say thanks to my daughters, Jennifer and Julie, for their support in this project and especially to my wife, Tammy, for holding down the fort while I was out skimming the treetops in Pave Lows and crunching through the brush with the Special Tactics Teams..

Alone MC-130H Combat Talon II clandestinely glides though the slipstream at 30,000 feet above enemy territory, its forward-looking infrared and array of electronic equipment constantly on the lookout for hostiles. Time hack, 0215; the pilot brings the aircraft to 12,000 feet. An arm shoots up into the air and the nomex-gloved hand spreads out, signaling to the team they are five minutes from the insertion point. Moments later the rear cargo ramp is lowered and five heavily laden figures in Battle Dress Uniform (BDU), SCUBA gear, and parachutes approach the opening. They huddle together, like an NFL team before the final play of the game. Last-minute checks are made, and equipment is tugged one more time. One member reaches down and gives a reassuring pat to the MP5-SD3 silenced submachine gun attached to his harness; another glances one last time at his altimeter.

GREEN . . . GREEN . . . GREEN, the jump light flashes and in a heartbeat all five men, as one, hurl themselves into the dark abyss that waits for them. Assuming a stable free-fall position, they are plummeting to the Earth's surface, now 11,000 feet below, at approximately 200 feet per second. The only sound heard is their breathing through the oxygen masks and the wind as it tears at their bodies and equipment. Moments turn into an eternity; then it is time. The altimeter now dictates that they transcend from their lofty flight and prepare to engage their RAPS, or ram-air parachute system. One final check of the altimeter and compass. As they reach the 3,500-foot point, one after the other pulls on the rip cord. Only the sounds of the canopy foils being deployed are heard by the team. In little more than two minutes after leaving the aircraft they are ready to steer toward their contact point.

In this case, though, it will not be some open drop zone (DZ) or even a small meadow in the middle of the forest. These men will land in the water and, after disposing of their parachutes, will continue on the mission underwater.

Using LAR-V rebreathers, the five specialists navigate underwater using an RJE compass board lit ever so slightly by a Cylamide chemical light stick. Their movement is invisible to anyone who may be on the surface, as the rebreathers emit no telltale bubbles to give them away. Flutter kicks are counted, and meter upon meter add up until they reach the shore line.

Silently the point man moves up onto the beach. Stops. Listens. Surveys the area. Listens again. After he is satisfied that they have arrived undetected, he directs his attention back to the sea and with deliberate, silent hand motions signals to the rest of the team. Slowly they emerge from the water and converge on the point man's position.

The team leader pulls out a global positioning system (GPS) and verifies the location and direction to the target. The information is passed on to the point man, who sets a compass heading and heads out. The team moves through the foliage and over the terrain like an invisible zephyr.

Who are these men?

They are not Navy SEALs, but they may have marked the area with infra-beacons before the frogmen fast-roped in. They are not U.S. Army Rangers, but before the Rangers ever executed an air drop on a drop zone this team might have been there for days.

You will not see them depicted in movies with guns blazing, or as the main characters in the latest Clancy novel. They prefer their anonymity and are often the unsung heroes of many covert operations. They are the men of the U.S. Air Force Special Operations Command, the Air Commandos, the Quiet Professionals. Their motto: ANYTIME, ANYWHERE.

Chapter 1

History of the Air Commandos

The origins of today's Air Force Special Operations Command can be traced back to the beginning of World War II. Aircrews and aircraft were used in the clandestine, unconventional, and psychological warfare roles in both the European and Pacific theaters of operation.

The Combat Talon of today would find its forerunner in the highly modified, paint-blackened B-24 "Liberator" bombers. These specialized B-24s were flown by members of the 801st Bombardment Group, Army Air Corps who were known as the Carpetbaggers. The crews of this unit, much like their current descendants, became proficient in flying low-level, long-range missions in terrain that was mostly mountains in poor weather and, of course, at night. These planes were instrumental in the delivery of covert agents, supplies, and psychological leaflets behind the enemy's lines.

The agents that would be parachuted into enemy-held territory were members of the Office of Strategic Services (OSS). Known as Jedburgh Teams, these teams generally consisted of three men and would link up with the partisan resistance fighters and organize and conduct guerrilla operations against the Germans in preparation of Operation Overlord.

In the early part of June 1944, six Jedburgh teams were parachuted into strategic locations in Brittany and France. There, units were successful in relaying critically needed intelligence in preparation for the Allied invasion of Normandy, on 6 June 1944—D-Day.

On another occasion, Air Corps special operations aircrews were tasked with the insertion of OSS agents into Yugoslavia, code name Halyard Mission. These agents, in connection with the partisans, arranged for the return of downed aircrews. Between June and August 1944 these OSS teams, along with help from the partisans, recovered more than 400 Americans and 80 Allied personnel. They were transported out on Air Corps C-47 transports from covert airfields.

World War II in the Pacific

While the OSS Jedburgh Teams were successfully conducting guerrilla operations in Europe, other aircrews were earning their namesake in the Pacific.

On 26 August 1943, General Henry H. "Hap" Arnold held a meeting with British Admiral Lord Louis Mountbatten to review plans for American air assistance of British commando operations in the China-Burma-India theater of operations. It was during this time that Gen. Arnold brought into being the concept of a new force. A highly mobile fighting unit, complete with its own transportation and logistics. This unit, which would exhibit the "can-do" spirit, would evolve into the No. 1 Air Commando Group. Gen. Arnold used the term *air commando* to honor Lord Mountbatten, who had previously commanded British commandos.

During its formation, this unit was initially designated Project 9, then Project CA 281. Later the name was changed to the 5318th Provisional Unit (Air), then once again to No. 1 Air Commando Force,

Veteran fighter pilots Lieutenant Colonels John Alison (left) and Philip Cochran are regarded as the driving force in the establishment of the air commandos. It was during their command that British "Chindit" commander, General Orde C. Wingate, penned them a letter stating, "Please be assured that we will go with your boys, any place, any time, any where." This became the motto for the Air Commandos and is still used in an abbreviated form by AFSOC today. *AFSOC*

The B-24 bomber was operated by the 801st Bombardment Group, nicknamed "the Carpetbaggers." This group specialized in covert air operations. An ancestor of today's Combat Talons, operating mostly at night, this highly modified, black-painted B-24 was used to deliver supplies, OSS agents, and leaflets behind enemy lines in Europe. *AFSOC*

and finally, the 1st Air Commando Group (1 ACG) in March 1944.

The task of forming this unit fell upon two veteran fighter pilots, Lieutenant Colonels Philip G. Cochran and John R. Alison. They were to build a self-sufficient highly motivated combat unit to support British Brigadier General Orde C. Wingate and his "Chindits" on long-range infiltrations into Burma, opposing the Japanese.

Cochran and Alison were designated co-commanders and given carte blanche by Gen. Arnold. Their orders were simple: ". . . I want the USAAF to spearhead Gen. Wingate's operation." Then the general gave them a further admonition: "To hell with the paperwork, go out and fight."

For such an organization there was no table of organization and equipment (TO&E). Under the highest priority given to them by Gen. Arnold, they were able to obtain the needed men and supplies to create the unit.

The task of manning the unit fell to Captain Robert E. Moist. Due to the covert nature of their mission, prospective candidates were given a minimal amount of information. No information regarding destination, but they were assured that missions would include combat. The attraction of combat and secrecy of the missions was enough to fill the ranks and made recruiting easy. In keeping with the nature of secrecy, the unit adopted the unofficial patch of a black question mark on a white circle.

With the manpower problem solved, Cochran and Alison now directed their attention to the aircraft needed to accomplish their mission. The inventory of aircraft grew and soon they had at their disposal C-47 Dakota Transports, CG-4A Waco gliders, P-51 Mustangs and P-47 Thunderbolt fighters, B-25 Mitchell bombers, UC-64 Norseman Utility aircraft, L-1 Vigilant and L-5 Sentinel Liaison planes, and for the first time in a combat environment, the YR-4 helicopter.

The air commandos flew over hazardous mountains and jungles to find and resupply the highly mobile British ground forces in hostile territory. Their success eventually led to the creation of two other such groups, the 2nd and 3rd ACGs.

The mission of the 1st Air Commando Group as defined by Gen. Arnold was to facilitate the forward movement of Wingate's troops, to supply and evacuate Wingate's force, to provide limited air covering and striking force, and to acquire air experience under the conditions expected to be encountered.

Arnold's air commandos performed a variety of conventional and unconventional combat as well as support missions deep behind enemy lines. The air commandos are credited with the first combat aircrew rescue by helicopter, multiple ground targets destroyed, and a number of enemy aircraft shot down.

On 15 February 1944, during a night training mission, an accident involving a C-47 Dakota and two Waco Gliders took the lives of four of Wingate's men as well as three Americans.

Such an incident could have easily shaken the men of the British force. On the following day, however, Wingate's commander sent a note to the air commandos reassuring their faith and trust in the unit's capability. The note read, "Please be assured that we will go with your boys Any Place, Any time, Any Where." This phrase became the motto of the 1st Air Commando Group and has been used in one variation or another in subsequent Air Commando

Paratroops prepare to load on C-47 of the 1st Air Commando Group (1 ACG) in 1944. These aircraft would support the British Chindits on long-range missions against the Japanese in the Burma theater of operations. *AFSOC*

The Air Commandos of World War II were the first to use the helicopter in a combat environment. Here an R-4 helicopter prepares to head out on a search-and-rescue mission in the jungles of Burma. *AFSOC*

units, as well as by today's Air Force Special Operations Command.

Post–World War II and Korea

With the end of World War II the U.S. military underwent many changes. The OSS evolved into the Central Intelligence Agency (CIA). The Army Air Corps became the United States Air Force, and the Air Commando Group was officially deactivated.

Officially, the U.S. Air Force no longer had an unconventional warfare capability. Unofficially, however, with the entrance of the United States into the Korean War, the USAF found itself again running clandestine operations, this time for the newly formed CIA. Under direction of the Military Air Transport Service (MATS) the Air Resupply and Communications Service (ARCS) was created on 28 February 1951. ARCS would be responsible for many of the covert operations of the war.

"Special air missions," as these operations were called, were as diverse as the pilots and aircraft that carried them out. Their inventory included SA-16 Albatross amphibians; modified B-29 bombers; C-47, C-54, C-118, and C-119 cargo planes; and H-19 helicopters.

The B-29 Superfortress served as a long-range insertion platform for covert teams. The B-29s were rigged to allow low-level insertion of agents and Special Forces teams. This was accomplished by removing the bottom rear gun turret and replacing it with a tub and hatch. When opened, this hatch would serve as a windbreak for the team parachuting out of the bomber. These crews would fly low-level (approximately 500 feet) to avoid enemy radar and visual detection, as usual operations were performed at night.

The Superfortress was also instrumental in the delivery of psychological warfare (PSYWAR) leaflets

During the Korean War the Air Force unconventional air operations used a number of airframes for their missions. The CIA, a successor to the OSS, used such aircraft as the B-29 for the incursion into both North and South Korea to deploy intelligence teams and supplies. *AFSOC*

and clandestine resupply of agents. Most of the B-29s were painted black to disappear against the night sky.

One of the unconventional special air missions was carried out by the secret unit known as Detachment 2 under the command of the Combined Command for Reconnaissance Activities, Korea (CCRAK).

Flying through the mountains of the Korean countryside without the benefit of forward looking infrared systems (FLIRs) and terrain-following radar, the crews inserted "Rabbits" behind the enemies lines. These agents were armed with SCR-300 radios and were to provide human intelligence (HUMINT). There was no planned extraction for these agents. Their only way back to base and safety was to walk.

The men of Detachment 2 were innovative and creative when it came to ways to wreak havoc on the enemy. Det 2 would be the first to use the C-47 as a bomber. By rigging the C-47 with special racks and latch points under the plane, the crews were able to sling two 75-gallon napalm canisters beneath the aircraft. Flying low and at night the crews would attack supply convoys moving from the north.

Det 2 also inserted agents that acted as a warning net to supply the Air Command with intelligence on the movement of Chinese and North Korean forces. Timing and terrain restrictions forced the Det 2 planner to be innovative again. The agents were issued smoke grenades that would signal enemy movement to the overflying C-47s. Red smoke indicated that the enemy had crossed that point. Green was used for close proximity of South Korean troops, and yellow meant no one had crossed. The method was crude but successful.

Another facet of Det 2 was the psychological warfare operations. Sometimes a pair of C-47s had loudspeakers inserted on board. The crews would then fly low over enemy positions. Other times the planes would drop PSYWAR leaflets on the enemy troops. These transports would be escorted by a flight of P-51 Mustangs to ensure that their messages would have the appropriate amount of backing.

The Korean War also brought out the importance of helicopter operations. Helicopter operations in 1952 were divided into two mission profiles. The 581st Air Resupply Squadron manning the new H-19A helicopters would run "BLACK HAT" ops (covert insertion of agents and Special Forces teams), while the 2157th Air Rescue Service would handle the "WHITE HAT" ops (combat air rescue).

There were times when the missions of these two units would overlap. On one occasion a U.S. Marine Corps F-4U Corsair was shot down behind enemy lines in North Korea. The pilot lay by his downed plane, wounded, getting colder by the minute, all the while being observed by North Korean troops. His wingmen strafed the area to keep the enemy soldiers from advancing on his position. The weather was closing in, they were running low on fuel and ammo, yet they still ran dummy strafing runs to keep the enemies' heads down. Extensive enemy gunfire succeeded in forcing the two F4Us from the crash site.

Although two Air Rescue H-19s were in the vicinity, low fuel prohibited them from reaching the downed flier. A helicopter from the Air Resupply unit, the "BLACK HAT" crew, was scrambled and headed immediately for the crash site.

Things were not looking good on the ground. With the wingmen gone, the North Koreans could now move in on the injured Marine pilot. The enemy began to rush his position. As they did, a flight of USAF F-80 jet fighters along with USMC Corsairs arrived overhead and began to decimate the enemy troops with 20-millimeter canon fire. While the fire fight was going on between the fighters and the North Koreans the H-19 extracted the pilot and raced from the scene.

An Air Commando A-1E "Sandy" sits ready on the tarmac on a base in South Vietnam. Ready to take off in support of the Jolly Greens on a search-and-rescue mission north of the DMZ, or wherever they were needed. *AFSOC*

An Air Commando A-1E Skyraider delivers a deadly napalm drop. Such a strike was a welcome sight over a beleaguered Special Forces camp. *AFSOC*

As their predecessors before them in World War II, those who flew and fought in Korea would pass along the heritage as they passed along their addition to the Air Commando legacy.

Cold War Era

With the end of the Korean War, the primary mission of the U.S. Air Force would be that of land-based bombers and intercontinental ballistic missiles of the Strategic Air Command. Once again, the Air Force's special operation would silently slip away into the shadows, until needed.

Throughout the fifties the Air Force was tasked with supporting anti-Communist rebellions.

One such rebellion was taking place in the small country of Tibet, where 80,000 guerrillas were giving the Chinese Communists a run for their money. The Chinese did have a real advantage that would be extremely difficult to counter: the terrain. The topology of Tibet did not lend itself to outside support. The West would have to sit this one out, or so the Chinese thought. Big mistake!

The intelligence community, still new to all these activities, did not have the resources or expertise to

The birth of a gunship. "Spooky," an AC-47 used in the Vietnam War, carried three 7.62-millimeter SUU-11A/1A minigun pods on the port side of the fuselage. These miniguns were capable of firing 3,000 or 6,000 rounds per minute. Using a banking maneuver, the pilot would perform a pylon turn over the target while the weapons were fired. Spooky was always a welcome sight when it arrived overhead of an isolated U.S. Army Green Beret outpost. *AFSOC*

carry out the missions. Help would come from the Air Force Detachment 2, 1045th Observations, Evaluation and Training Group. Special air missions were on again!

Plans for covert airdrops of weapons, supplies, and personnel were formulated and assets were arranged. One problem loomed large on the planner's horizon, the Tibetan geography.

The distance was far, the altitude extremely high. For example, lowlands in Tibet were a pleasant 13,000 feet. Fundamental to the success of these missions was finding a suitable aircraft with the adequate range and payload capability.

The obvious choice was the new Lockheed C-130 Hercules; however, the only Air Force unit flying the 130s was the 315th Air Division in the Pacific. Enter the Office of Special Operation (OSO) under the direction of the secretary of defense and charged with supporting the intelligence community. Detachment 2 got their needed aircraft; the C-130s were made available for the missions.

When the planes arrived at Detachment 2 they were stripped of all "USAF" markings. The crew were to fly the 130s "sterile." They flew into Tibet from Thailand across miles of uncharted mountain ranges relying mostly on the skill of the navigator using celestial guides.

An average mission might carry supplies rigged for the air drop or parachute-trained Tibetan guerrilla with a U.S. advisor. As confidence and experience grew, Det 2 became more innovative and was able to provide the critical air support to the guerrillas. The new Hercules aircraft were often pushed to their limits on the mountain ranges of Tibet. During this entire campaign, not one plane or crew member was lost.

Vietnam

Early on in the sixties, the Cold War began to heat up, primarily in Third World countries where Communist-led insurgents introduced a violent movement to those areas. Known as Wars of Liberation, they sprung up all around the globe. Obviously, this caused great concern in the United States and other Western nations.

President John F. Kennedy had developed an interest in counterinsurgency, the method of defeating guerrilla movements. He would go on to say, "There is another type of war, new in its intensity, ancient in its origins—war by guerrillas, subversives, insurgents, assassins, war by ambush instead of combat. . . ." President Kennedy recognized a need for a force, a "special" force to counter this threat.

The Air Force response came in the spring of 1961, when General Curtis E. LeMay, Air Force chief of staff, directed the creation of the 4400th Combat Crew Training Squadron (CCTS), code named "Jungle Jim." Located at Eglin Air Force Base, Auxiliary Field #9 (Hurlburt Field), the 4400th CCTS started its journey into the annals of Special Warfare history with 352 officers and men and a total inventory of 32 aircraft (16 C-47 Transports, 8 B-26 bombers, and 8 T-28 Trainers).

The mission of the 4400th CCTS was to provide close air support for Special Forces behind enemy lines and counterinsurgency training. The CCTS developed Foreign Internal Defense (FID) tactics and techniques for building a counterinsurgency capability in numerous Third World countries.

Later that year, in November 1961, Detachment 2 of the 4400th CCTS, code name "Farm Gate," deployed to the Republic of South Vietnam. They were to become the first Air Force unit to conduct actual combat operations in Vietnam. The official Air Force mission was to train South Vietnamese pilots.

The AC-119 "Stinger" was used in the early evolution in gunships. A converted cargo plane, the C-119 "Flying Boxcar" was fitted with two 20-millimeter chain cannons, along with a large radar dome that guided the firepower to the target. By the end of 1969 the 14th Air Commando Wing had 16 AC-119G Shadows and 12 AC-119K Stinger gunships operating throughout Vietnam. *AFSOC*

In addition to the massive firepower, the AC-130A was fitted with forward-looking infrared (FLIR), LLLTV (low light level television), an AN/ASD-S direction finder, AVQ-18 laser designator/range-finder, radar pods, and a searchlight. These electronic modifications allowed the Spectre crew to mete out a devastating blow to any hostile ground force. *AFSOC*

Hostilities escalated faster than the original role would permit, however. "Farm Gate's" primary ground attack aircraft was the T-28 trainer. Approximately 400 were converted to the Air Forces needs and specifications for the job at hand. The T-28s of Det 2 were powered by 1,425-horsepower Wright engines driving a three-blade prop. The new planes designated T-28D-5 had in-wing ammunitions, tow underwing .50-caliber machine guns, and six bomb racks. Two gunpods and four bomb racks were located on a reinforced undercarriage. The planes could accommodate napalm, general-purpose bombs, fragmentation grenades, rockets, and parachute flares. These T-28s would also see action with the "Ravens" in the secret war in Laos.

As the war in Vietnam expanded, so did the role of the Air Force's special operation forces. Gen. LeMay responded to this in the expansion of the 440th CCTS to the Special Air Warfare Center (SAWC) at Eglin in April 1962. SWAC consisted of the 1st Air Commando Group, 1st Air Combat Applications Group, and a combat support group. To assist the new organization, the Air Force created a new "counterinsurgency" office specialty code. It was overwhelming that in an era of nuclear weapons and space missions, SAWC had more interest and volunteers than anyone could have imagined.

The Special Air Warfare Center added to its catalogue such aircraft as the O-1 and O-2 observation planes, A-37 and A-1 attack fighters, and C-46, C-119, C-123, and later C-130 cargo aircraft, along with several types of helicopters.

In May 1963, the 1st Air Commando Group was redesignated the 1st Air Commando Wing. Operational strength rose from 2,665 to 3,000 and the squadrons increased to six. In the tradition of their predecessors, the Vietnam-era Air Commandos developed tactics and techniques that earned their exploits an honored place in Air Force Special Operations heritage.

In 1964 the Air Commando Squadron traded its T-28s for the A-1E Skyraider. Often referred to as the "flying dump truck," it had a range of more than 1,100 miles and could loiter over a target for hours. The Skyraider was 40 feet long with a wingspan of 50 feet. Power was generated by a 2,700-horsepower Wright HP engine. The A-1E could carry an ordnance load of 12,000 pounds of bombs, rockets, or napalm canisters. It also mounted four 20-millimeter cannons.

Missions began to change for the squadrons, from training South Vietnamese pilots to the direct combat action of air support for U.S. ground forces throughout Vietnam. The Air Commandos and their Skyraiders became a common sight for many a downed pilot, as the "Sandys" or "Spads" (nicknames for the A-1E) were called upon to assist with search-and-rescue (SAR) operations.

In 1965, the 1st Air Commando squadron was awarded the Presidential Unit Citation, the first such USAF award since the Korean War. This recognition was not without a price as 40 Air Commandos gave their lives in the service of their country.

The Air Commandos were masters in improvising and innovation. Such an example can be seen in

Tracers light up the sky over a city in South Vietnam. The pattern of the Spectre gunship can be seen as thousands of 7.62-millimeter rounds from the gunship's miniguns fire in support of the troops below. *AFSOC*

the conversion of the well-flown C-47. The transport had been in service with the Air Commandos since World War II; however, the war in Vietnam called for ideas in dealing with the elusive Vietcong guerrillas. In the tradition of the "Carpetbaggers," the men of the 1st Air Commando Squadron at Bien Hoa began working on the conversion of the C-47 Dakota, into the AC-47 Gunship. Nicknamed "Puff the Magic Dragon" due to its impressive nighttime fire-breathing capabilities, the official call sign was "Spooky." The "Spooky" emblem is still in use today with the current Spectre crews of the Air Force Special Operations Command.

Aptly named, the AC-47 would surely bring an eerie display to the enemy who would come under its massive firepower. The AC-47 Gunship was equipped with three General Electric SUU-11A/A Gatling miniguns capable of firing 6,000 rounds-per-minute of 7.62-millimeter bullets on the port side of the aircraft. The plane would carry 24,000 rounds of conventional ammunitions along with 45 flares that could be dropped in an area where they would hang suspended by parachutes for up to three minutes. The AC-47 had a crew of six: pilot/AC, copilot, navigator, and three gunners. The pilot would bank the plan into a pylon turn and run a "racetrack" around the ground position to be attacked. Flying at 120 knots in a 3,000-foot circle, the AC-47 was capable of placing a 7.62-millimeter round in every square inch of a football field–sized target in three seconds.

By fall of 1965 20 gunships were deployed with the 4th Air Commando Squadron. Their mission: to

Sikorsky HH-3, the Air Force's Jolly Green Giant helicopter, with jungle hoist and fuel probe. These helicopters were responsible for plucking many a downed airman from the grasp of the Vietcong and NVA during the Vietnam War. Nothing would give a downed pilot a greater feeling of relief than to hear a Jolly overhead and see that jungle penetrator plunge through the foliage. These HH-3s were later fitted with 7.62-millimeter miniguns to aid the helicopter crews and PJs in suppressing ground fire and completing their task of extraction.

provide close air support with flares and fire power to hamlets under night attack and to supplement strike aircraft supporting friendly forces. The AC-47 became a welcome sight over many U.S. Army Special Forces (Green Beret) outposts during the height of the conflict.

The next progression in gunship modification was the conversion of the C-119 "Flying Boxcar." The 71st Special Operations Squadron took delivery of the first AC-119G model gunships in January 1969, call sign "Shadow." The AC-119Gs carried four of the 7.62-millimeter miniguns, which delivered rounds with deadly accuracy. By the end of 1969 the 14th Air Commando Wing had 16 AC-119G Shadows and 12 AC-119K Stinger gunships operating throughout Vietnam. The K model had the addition of two 20-millimeter Chain Cannon, along with a large radar dome, which guided the firepower to the target.

During the seven-week siege of U.S. Army Special Forces camps at Dak Pek and Dak Seang, the AC-119 proved indispensable as the Air Commandos flew 147 sorties in support of the SF camps. More than

2 million rounds of 7.62-millimeter and 22,000 rounds of 20-millimeter cannon shells were expended in defending these two Green Beret outposts.

While enormous amounts of ordnance was to be expended in the support of these remote camps, another matter came to the attention of the Air Commandos: resupplying the defenders. The Army used C-7 Caribou transports to resupply the SF camps and regularly took enemy fire. After the downing of the third Caribou, the pilots of the C-7s and the AC-119s got together to conceive a new battle tactic. The resupply tactics worked as follows: The AC-119s would lay suppressive fire around the camp until the A-7 reached its drop point. The AC-119 would then cease fire and light up the drop zone (DZ) with its illuminator. The DZ would look like a night game in the World Series and the Caribous would deliver the parachute-rigged supplies into the DZ. Once the drop was made, the C-7 crew would call for "lights out" and disappear into the night. This tactic was employed during the seven-week siege at the two SF camps 68 times without losing one aircraft to enemy fire. In the end, the camps held.

With the aging of the AC-47 and AC-119 series of gunships, the Air Force sought a replacement. The air platform of choice was the C-130. In 1968 the Lockheed Hercules first evaluated would be so heavily laden with weapons and sensors that it was designated Project Gunboat. That term would slowly disappear as the AC-130 became to officially be referred to as the AC-130A "Spectre" gunship. Webster's dictionary defines *spectre* as 1. an apparition; 2. any object of terror or dread. The U.S. Air Force defines it as 1. a predator; 2. one that goes out looking for trouble.

The AC-130 Spectre gunship carried more than the four 7.62-millimeter miniguns and upgraded to four 20-millimeter M-61 Vulcan Chain Cannons. Along with this rather impressive array of firepower, the AC-130s were packed to the gills with advanced electronic devices. The night observation device, or NOD, was an image light intensifier that magnified the moon and star light to enable the NOD operator a clear view of ground activity. A FLIR system was installed to pick up heat signatures from both humans and vehicles, regardless of the lighting conditions. A fire-control computer was installed, linking the gunsight, sensors and guns into a coordinated weapon system. A steerable illuminator was mounted on the port side, which consisted of two 20kW Xenon arc lamps capable of giving off visible, infrared, or ultraviolet light. These early AC-130 gunships were operated by the newly formed 16th Special Operations Squadron, attached to the 6th Tactical Fighter Wing at Ubon Royal Thai Air Force Base.

Subsequent Spectres would receive major modification in armament. The eight weapons pods were replaced with two 20-millimeter Gatling guns and two 40-millimeter Bofors cannons. Enhancement to electronics came in low-light-level television (LLLTV) and improved infared (IR) equipment, all of which allowed better night vision and detection capability. The two 20kW illuminators were replaced with low-power 2kW units; this lessened

the chances of a surface-to-air missile (SAM) locking onto the signature. Black Crow (BC) devices were also installed to pick up the electromagnetic radiation emissions from the NVA trucks ignitions systems.

A fully equipped Spectre could carry a crew of 13 to 14. Among them were five navigators, one who acted as the Electric Warfare (EW) officer. His task was to man the BC and defensive systems of the aircraft. One navigator would be on the flight deck with the pilot, co-pilot, and flight engineer. The other three navigators along with an EW officer made up the Sensor Team and occupied "the booth," a small section inside the cargo compartment of the Hercules. They would view the world outside the aircraft via television screens and sensor monitors. Joining them would be the fire control officer and three other crew members who would operate the LLLTV, IR, or BC sensors. The LLLTV unit was located on the port side of the aircraft forward of the 20-millimeter cannons. This device could amplify the existing light 60,000 times and produce television images as if it were noon. In the same position as the LLLTV was the Pave Way I laser designator. This designator provided a pulse beam for guiding laser munitions. The IR console produced images registering heat emissions. Cool objects appeared black or gray, while heated items, such as the engine of a truck moving down the trail, showed up white. If one were to look into the "booth" you would see numerous crew members concentrating on various monitors and hands poised on joysticks, similar to those used by PC gamers.

The new Spectres were assigned to the 16th SOS. The mission: to seek and destroy enemy trucks infiltrating supplies down the Ho Chi Minh Trail. By March 1969, the Spectres accounted for 44 percent of the trucks destroyed in a 30-day period. Feeling the pinch, the North Vietnamese upped the ante by increasing air defenses on the trail by 400 percent. Not to be outbid, the Spectre received some upgrading of its own. In February 1972 the first AC-130 was equipped with a 105-millimeter Howitzer. This

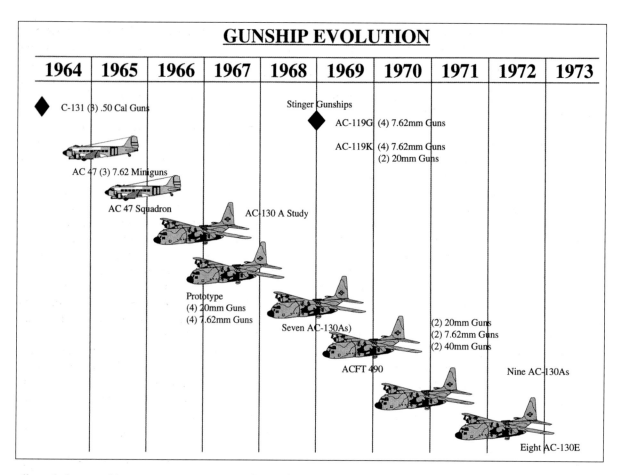

GUNSHIP EVOLUTION

1964	1965	1966	1967	1968	1969	1970	1971	1972	1973

C-131 (3) .50 Cal Guns

Stinger Gunships

AC-119G (4) 7.62mm Guns

AC-119K (4) 7.62mm Guns
(2) 20mm Guns

AC 47 (3) 7.62 Miniguns

AC 47 Squadron

AC-130 A Study

Prototype
(4) 20mm Guns
(4) 7.62mm Guns

Seven AC-130As)

(2) 20mm Guns
(2) 7.62mm Guns
(2) 40mm Guns

ACFT 490

Nine AC-130As

Eight AC-130E

allowed the gunship to engage targets on the trail from a greater stand-off distance.

U.S. Air Force data confirms that the top three truck killers on the trail were the AC-130, AC-119, and the F-4 Phantoms. During the 1969–1970 "truck hunting season," 20,000 trucks were reported damaged or destroyed. The last mission for the AC-130 would take place over the jungles of Cambodia on 15 August 1973.

The 16th SOS returned to the United States in December 1975. The H models were based out of Hurlburt Field, 1st Special Operations Wing. A models went to the Air Force Reserve 711th SOS at Duke Field. The Spectres carried on at their new homes,

waiting to be called upon again. It would be five years before the Pentagon revisited the Spectre's capabilities, shortly after the Iran hostage rescue disaster at Desert One in 1980.

Vietnam was referred to as the "Helicopter War." Hueys, Cobras, Chinooks, Slicks, and Dust-offs, they brought you in, they supplied you, and they took you out. U.S Air Force helicopters played a vital role in a war where there were no front lines. In a war where the entire country was "the" battle zone, Air Force helicopter crews found themselves rescuing downed pilots in North Vietnam one day and inserting an SF team in Laos or Cambodia the next.

While the Air Force did use the ubiquitous UH-1 Huey for assorted tasks, the helicopter that became synonymous with Air Force Special Operations in Vietnam was the Sikorsky HH-3, the "Jolly Green Giant." In November 1965 the first Sikorsky HH-3E arrived in the Republic of South Vietnam. These helicopters were armored and had the capability to mount weapons systems. The HH-3E also had a unique feature for a helicopter; it was equipped with an in-flight refueling probe. Remote areas were now accessible to air rescue service crews and their Jolly Greens. Additional equipment for the HH-3E included rescue hoists and self-sealing fuel tanks. Maximum speed was 162 miles per hour with a range of 465 miles.

As the war escalated, so did the need for a finely tuned rescue unit. In January 1966, having been baptized in fire and their combat skills honed, the ARS was redesignated the ARRS—Air Rescue and Recovery Service.

This new unit was also given a new aircraft to supplement the HH-3Es. The Sikorsky HH-53C "Super Jolly" entered service with the ARRS in 1968. Based on the Sikorsky S-65 Sea Stallion, used by the U.S. Marines as a heavy lift assault chopper, the Super Jolly became the Air Force's premiere combat rescue aircraft.

The HH-53 was a formidable aircraft and weapons system. Powered by two General Electric T-64/GE 413 turboshafts rated at 3,925 shaft horsepower (each) gave the helicopter a maximum speed of 170 knots. Internally it would carry 450 gallons of aviation fuel, with the capability of mounting external fuel tanks on the sponsons, which would carry 3,415 gallons of fuel. It was equipped with a fully retractable landing gear, even though it had a watertight hull due to it origins being based on the sea-going USMC platform. The pilots sat in titanium-armored, bat-wing seats, and metal plate armor was in the floor of the nose. Its powerful rescue hoist was mounted in the starboard cabin door, equipped with 250 feet of cable and fitted with a "jungle penetrator." The rear-loading ramp could be opened in flight allowing the insertion of SF teams, or engaging one of the GAU-2A six-barreled 7.62 miniguns. The other was mounted near the forward winch. Normal crew for the Super Jolly was pilot, co-pilot, flight engineer, who could act as winch operator and gunner, and usually two PJs, pararescue specialists.

One of the more famous USAF-supported special operations missions was the Son Tay raid in 1970. Air Force Special Operations assets played a critical role in the attempted rescue of U.S. prisoners of war, planned by Colonel "Bull" Simmons. Although no prisoners were found, the mission was executed flawlessly by both Air Force and Army Special Operation Forces.

During the Vietnam War the Air Commandos would never account for more than five percent of the U.S. Air Force personnel "in country." Yet, their dedication and courage was recognized in the fact that out of the 12 Air Force Medals of Honor, 5 would be awarded to members of the U.S. Air Force Special Operations.

As the Vietnam War began winding down, special operations forces (SOF) capability progressively declined as well. In June 1974, the Air Force USAFSOF was redesignated the 834th Tactical Composite Wing (TCW), effectively bringing to a close the most aggressive, far-reaching effort by the USAF to support unconventional warfare. In July 1975, the 834th TCW was renamed the 1st Special Operations Wing (1 SOW), and by 1979 it was the only SOF wing.

What began as a noble attempt by the United States special operations forces ended in tragedy in the darkness of an Iranian desert. It was April 1980 when Special Forces Operation Detachment Delta, better known as "Delta Force," along with its Air Force and Marine aircrews, met with disaster. What Colonel "Charging" Charlie Beckwith did not know at the time was that the operation was headed toward disaster from the onset. Over the years there have been investigations, hearings, and countless articles written on why the mission ended in a debacle, so we will not belabor the issue here. All the Monday-morning quarterbacks had one conclusion in common, however, Operation Eagle Claw failed. This cost the lives of eight gallant troops, it cost the honor of the United States of America, and it hurt the credibility of U.S. special operations.

The Navy helicopters with Marine pilots proved to be the Achilles' heel of Operation Eagle Claw. One can only speculate on the compilations of mishaps that besieged the Sea Stallion helicopters. Some got lost in the desert and others malfunctioned, leaving the anxious force without the adequate airlift capability necessary to accomplish the rescue attempt. From the inception of the plan they were "the" weak link. Were the pilots up to the task?

The Marine pilots, if we look at today's standards, had big boots to fill. They were being asked to fly at night. This alone was unusual practice for the "flying leathernecks." These pilots were now being asked to perform the extraordinary: launch off the deck of a carrier, at night, fly NOE (nape of the earth) where radar could not detect them, and use no running lights. The pilots were issued PVS5 night vision goggles; however, they could be worn only at 30-minute intervals. This meant the pilot and co-pilot had to alternate flying the huge helicopter every 30 minutes. The Marines had no pilots that had been trained in this type of flying. In fact, none of the service branches were prepared for such a contingency.

Following the disaster at Desert One, a review committee known as the Holloway Commission convened to look into problems within U.S. special operations. The outcome of this commission resulted in two major recommendations. First, the Department of Defense should establish a Counterterrorism Joint Task Force (CTJTF) as a field organization of the Joint Chiefs of Staff (JCS) with a permanently assigned staff and forces. The JCS would plan, train for, and conduct operations to counter terrorist activities directed against the United States. The CTJTF would use military forces in the counterterrorism (CT) role. These forces could range in size from small units of highly specialized personnel to larger integrated forces. Second, the JCS should consider the formation of a Special Operations Advisory Panel (SOAP). This panel would consist of high-ranking officers to be drawn from both active service and retired personnel. The prerequisite for selection was a background in special operations or having served as a commander in chief (CINC) or JCS level and having maintained a

---

In addition to providing air support for U.S. Special Operation Forces, AFSOC provided ATC and pararescue capabilities for USSOCOM. Here Staff Sergeant Bob Benton of the 23rd Special Tactics Squadron pauses and watches over his team as they take a break from patrolling through the dense jungle. He is armed with an M-4 with M203 40-millimeter grenade launcher in hand, ready for instant use.

Hurlburt Field, located on the west end of Eglin Air Force Base, is the home of the U.S. Air Force Special Operations Command.

proficient level of interest in special operations or defense policy.

The mission of the SOAP would be to review and evaluate highly classified special operations planning to provide an independent assessment. Consequently, the progressive reorganization and resurgence of United States special operation forces began.

While this was occurring, the Air Force transferred responsibility for Air Force special operations from Tactical Air Command (TAC) to Military Airlift Command (MAC) in December 1982. The commander of the 23rd Air Force at Scott Air Force Base, Illinois, would assume all control of the Air Force special operations units. This new numbered Air

Force was tasked with the worldwide missions of special operations, combat rescue, pararescue training, medical evacuation, and training of HC-130 and helicopter crewmen.

Subsequently, on 1 March 1983, in response to the Holloway Commission Report, all U.S. Air Force special operation forces were consolidated into the 1st Special Operations Wing (SOW) at Hurlburt Field, Florida. The 1st SOW would direct and coordinate active and reserve components of the Special Operation Squadrons (SOS). Active components consisted of the 8th SOS operating MC-130 Combat Talons and HC-130 Hercules Tankers, the 16th SOS operating AC-130 Spectre gunships, and the 20th

SOS operating the MH-53 Pave Low and HH-53 Jolly Green Giant helicopters. The 1720th Special Tactics Group provided the combat control teams.

Reserve components of Air Force special operation forces included the 919th Special Operations Group (SOG) operating AC-130A gunships, the 302nd SOG operating the EC-130E command and control aircraft, and the Pennsylvania Air National Guard flying the Volant Solo EC-130E Psychological Operations aircraft.

In addition to traditional special operations skills, the 23rd conducted weather reconnaissance, security support for intercontinental ballistic missile sites, and training of USAF helicopter and HC-130 crewmen.

Operation URGENT FURY

In October 1983, 23rd AF participated with other Caribbean forces in the successful rescue of Americans from the island nation of Grenada. During the seven-day operation, centered at Point Salines Airport, 23rd AF furnished MC-130s, AC-130s, an EC-130 aircraft, aircrews, maintenance, and support people.

During the Grenada operation the 1st Special Operations Wing had two missions. MC-130 Combat Talons were tasked with delivering U.S. Army Rangers to Point Salines, while Spectre gunships provided the air-to-ground support fire. Combat controllers of the 23rd and 24th Special Tactics Squadron were air-dropped in with the U.S. Army Rangers at Port Salinas airport, making an unprecedented combat jump from only 500 feet. Each controller was laden with parachute gear and more than 90 pounds of mission-critical equipment. Upon landing they quickly established a command and control radio net. They carried out air traffic operations for follow-on forces both at the airport and other in-country missions. In addition to this, the combat control teams (CCT) performed as forward air control (FAC) for Air Force Spectre gunships, Navy fighters, and Army helicopter gunships.

Throughout the operation the crews of the 1st SOW continued in the tradition of the Air Commandos who preceded them. Flying in numerous sorties and fire missions they performed mission after mission. During the entire operations, they sustained no casualties.

The Grenada operation was not without its cost to the special operations community. Four U.S. Navy SEALs were lost at sea during a Rubber Duck insertion. This tragedy hit the SOF community hard. Operation Urgent Fury was also fraught with planning problems from the get-go. A lack of standardization for the special operation assets contributed to this plan gone awry.

Special operations forces in Grenada did have a few rough edges; however, most of these planning problems were overcome as the special operations personnel from all three service branches excelled at what they do best: improvise, adapt, and overcome to achieve their missions' goals.

The Grenada mission was the springboard for the further consolidation of U.S. Special Operations Forces. The Air Force particularly took a proactive stance to rebuild a powerful special operations force. In May 1986, Congressman William Cohen, Senator Sam Nunn, and Congressman Dan Daniel introduced legislation that formed the basis to amend the 1986 Defense Authorizations Bill. This bill, signed into law in October 1986, in part directed the formation of a unified command responsible for special operations. In April 1987, the U.S. Special Operations Command (USSOCOM) was established at MacDill Air Force Base, Florida, and Army General James J. Lindsay assumed command. Four months later, 23rd Air Force moved to Hurlburt Field.

In August 1989, General Duane H. Cassidy, MAC commander in chief, divested all nonspecial operations units from the 23rd Air Force. Consequently, the 23rd Air Force served in a dual role—reporting to MAC, but also functioning as the air component to USSOCOM.

Operation JUST CAUSE

On 20 December 1989, at 0100 local, the United States launched an attack on Panama. The objectives of the attack were to protect U.S. personnel and installations, neutralize the Panamanian Defense Force, and capture General Manuel Noriega. During this operation the Air Force special operations units saw extensive use. Due to the surgical firing capability, the Spectres were the ideal solution for the close-in urban combat environment with limited collateral damage. The Spectres were launched from the 16th Special Operations Squadron ("Ghostriders") at Hurlburt Field, Florida.

Other Air Force special operations assets included an EC-130 from the 193rd ANG stationed at the Harrisburg Airport, Pennsylvania, to perform psychological warfare operations during the invasion. Pararescuemen and CCTs participated in operations with the U.S. Army's 75th Rangers at Torrijos Airfield and Rio Hato Air Base. Combat Controllers would also be attached to U.S. Navy SEAL Team 4 in support of the frogmen as they assaulted Paitilla Airport and disabled General Noriega's personal jet.

In retrospect, Operation Just Cause served as a proving ground for the 1991 war in the Middle East. Night tactics and stealth weapons were battle tested in Panama and later accounted for many of the successes in Desert Storm. While not quite the fiasco of the Grenadian assault in 1983, Operation Just Cause did have some serious problems. Talk to the SEALs who survived the raid at Paitilla Airport. The invasion of Panama also established a strategy in the way U.S. Special Operation Forces were deployed and used in the future.

The Birth of U.S. Air Force Special Operations Command (AFSOC)

On 22 May 1990, General Larry D. Welch, Air Force chief of staff, redesignated 23rd Air Force as Air Force Special Operations Command (AFSOC). AFSOC became responsible for the combat readiness of Air Force Special Operations forces. Headquartered at Hurlburt Field, Florida, the group reports directly to the Air Force chief of staff and is the Air Force's component of the U.S. Special Operations Command.

The new major command consisted of three wings, the 1st, 39th, and 353rd Special Operations Wings, as well as the 1720th Special Tactics Group, the U.S. Air Force Special Operations School, and the Special Missions Operational Test and Evaluation Center. The Air Reserve components included the 919th Special Operations Group (Air Force Reserve) at Duke Field, Florida, and the 193rd SOG (Air National Guard) at Harrisburg Airport, Pennsylvania.

Today, having undergone further evolutions, AFSOC has approximately 12,500 active, reserve, and national guard personnel, 20 percent of whom are stationed overseas. The command owns more than 100 fixed- and rotary-wing aircraft, divided among one wing, the 16th SOW, and two groups, the 352nd and 353rd SOG. This configuration epitomizes the consolidated wing/group concept.

AFSOC is the Air Force element of the United States Special Operation Command (USSOCOM). Its mission is to provide mobility, surgical firepower, covert tanker support, and Special Tactics Teams. These units will normally operate in concert with U.S. Army and U.S. Navy special operation forces, including Special Forces, Rangers, Special Operations Aviation Regiment, SEAL teams, psychological operations (PYSOP) forces, and Civil Affairs units. AFSOC supports a wide range of activities from combat operations of a limited duration to longer-term conflicts. They also provide support to foreign governments and their military. Dependent on shifting priorities, AFSOC maintains a flexible profile allowing it to respond to numerous missions.

AFSOC is committed to continual improvement to provide Air Force special operations forces for worldwide deployment and assignment to regional linked commands to conduct unconventional warfare, direct action, special reconnaissance, personnel recovery, counterterrorism, foreign internal defense,

"Fill 'er up." Two MH-60 Pave Hawks extend their refueling probes and take on fuel from an MH-130P Combat Shadow. AFSOC provided USSOCOM the required air support to carry out special operations missions worldwide. *AFSOC*

psychological operations, and collateral special operations activities.

Unconventional warfare (UW) encompasses guerrilla warfare, the use of irregular forces, normally indigenous personnel operating in enemy-held territory, and other direct-offensive, low-visibility, covert operations. Incorporated in the UW mission are the indirect activities: subversion, sabotage, intelligence gathering, and evasion and escape. Armed rebellion against an established force or occupying power is often within the scope of UW. In wartime AFSOC may be tasked with directly supporting any resistance or guerrilla force. Commonly this is accomplished by infiltrating operational units, such as a U.S. Army A-

Team, into denied or sensitive areas for the purpose of training, equipping, and advising or directing indigenous forces.

Direct action (DA) involves small-scale offensive actions, normally of a short duration, conducted by Special Tactic Squadron (STS) teams. Such actions include seizure, destroying, capture of enemy personnel, any action that would inflict damage on enemy personnel or material. STS units are highly trained and may employ raids, ambushes, and other small unit tactics in the pursuit of these mission goals. They may use mines and other demolitions, or conduct attacks by employing fire support from air, ground, or sea assets. Direct action may find the STS

29

The AFSOC headquarters building at Hurlburt Field, Florida. The three crests are those of the U.S. Air Force, U.S. Special Operations Command, and AFSOC. Upon entering the lobby you are greeted by two very serious AFSOC security police. There you wait until they decide if you can go any farther.

team providing thermal guidance for precision-guided "smart bombs." One such DA that is the STS forte is airfield seizure. Put an STS team on the ground, couple them with a company of Rangers, place a Spectre overhead, and you've seized yourself one enemy airfield. This is a gross understatement, but once you see it put together, the Air Commandos make it look like a textbook operation. Jumping in with the Rangers, the CCT will establish the airhead, setup air traffic control, and provide CAS from Spectre gunships and Pave Low helicopters. While the assault progresses, PJs will provide triage and medical support to the assault force. There are few nations in the world capable of repelling a combined force of Rangers and STTs; you do not want to be on the receiving end of a DA op.

Special reconnaissance (SR) is defined as the reconnaissance and surveillance activity conducted by AFSOC units. Conducted by STS teams, this covers the area of HUMINT. SR places U.S. "eyes on target" in hostile, denied, or politically sensitive territory. An STS team could be tasked to conduct these missions. This means putting warm bodies on the ground in a specific location to accomplish what no satellite is

capable of accomplishing. Reconnaissance and surveillance, or R&S, will infiltrate into enemy area to report back to their commanders necessary information needed to carry ongoing attacks. STS teams may be used to acquire or verify, by visual observation or other methods available, information concerning the capabilities, intentions, and activities of an enemy force. Special reconnaissance includes meteorological, hydrographic, and geographic characteristics of the objective area. Additionally, SR includes target acquisition, bomb damage assessment (BDA), and poststrike reconnaissance. Reconnaissance provides the command with intelligence or "the answers" needed to conduct operations.

Special reconnaissance provides intelligence that is:
- *strategic*—data that is required by national decision-makers in formulating national or foreign defense policies.
- *operational*—these details and reports are provided to theater-level commanders to plan and conduct their campaigns.
- *tactical*—information that commanders need to fight battles.

Furthermore, SR may result in the request for a regional survey. Regional survey teams (RST), on the other hand, would be put on location in the absence of hostilities. This may be prior to an assault to give the CINC a clearer picture of the DZ, landing zone (LZ), or assault zone. This can be accomplished by surveying the assault zone with special cameras using a small video diskette. This diskette is then read into a reader that can convert video images into computer images (files), which can be sent back to assault team planners to actually "see" what the team on the ground is looking at and make their evaluation.

Counterterrorism (CT) consists of the offensive actions taken to prevent, deter, and respond to terrorism. This includes intelligence gathering and threat analysis. In support of CT operations AFSOC fixed-wing and rotary aircraft are ideal for such missions.

Pave Lows helicopters are designed to deliver SOF troops through any terrain, in any kind of weather, day or night. Spectre gunships provide highly accurate and mobile firepower. Such assets could be on station in the rapidly changing environment of a CT operation. The fact that AFSOC aircraft are refuelable enhances the flexibility and reduces the reaction time in meeting the critical demands of such an undertaking.

Foreign internal defense (FID) is a primary means of providing U.S. military special operation forces expertise to other governments in support of their internal defense and developmental efforts. By providing such training, special operations forces may preclude the deployment or combat involving conventional forces in a particular region of the world.

Psychological operations (PSYOP) have turned the tide of many battles without firing a single shot. AFSOC is capable of conducting these operations in conjunction with other special operation missions or in support of SOF forces. AFSOC can support strategic, operations, tactical, or consolidated PSYOP objectives. Using specially configured aircraft, PSYOP objectives can be achieved by providing intelligence, leaflet distribution, or media broadcasts.

Collateral special operations activities include security activities, counter-drug operations personnel recovery, coalition support, and other special activities as they arise. These are missions in which SOF personnel are not normally trained, organized, and equipped.

Combat search and rescue (CSAR) is where the PJs put their creed, "That Others May Live," on the line. CSAR differs from a standard search and rescue mission in the fact that you do not have the luxury of time. A conventional rescue may allow you to mend casualties on site and evacuate the injured. With a CSAR you have to locate, stabilize, and move out fast, most likely under enemy fire. When seconds may cost the life of a downed pilot or air crew, the STS team springs into action. Mission parameters are drawn up and evaluated: How many friendlies are down? How many enemy troops are in the vicinity? How much time will they need to get to the downed

pilot or aircraft? How much time on target will they need? Will the CSAR take place at night or in daylight? And the list goes on until the STS group is satisfied that all options have been considered and the forces to complete the mission are in place. Ninety-nine percent of the time such an operation will include a security force, or "shooters," as the STS calls them. These shooters may be U.S. Army Rangers, U.S. Army Special Forces, or U.S. Navy SEALs. Such a formidable force ensures the highest probability of a successful rescue.

16th Special Operations Wing
Located at Hurlburt Field, the 16th Special Operations Wing is the oldest and most experienced unit in AFSOC. It includes the 6th Special Operations Squadron, which is responsible for the SOW's aviation foreign internal defense unit; the 4th SOS, which operates the AC-130U Spectre gunships; the 8th SOS, which flies the MC-130E Combat Talon; the 15th SOS, with the MC-130H Combat Talon II; the 16th SOS, equipped with the AC-130H Spectre gunship; and the 20th SOS, which flies the MH-53J Pave Low III helicopter. The 9th SOS, located at nearby Eglin Air Force Base flies the HC-130N/P Combat Shadow

352nd Special Operations Group
Stationed overseas at RAF Mildenhall, United Kingdom, is the designated Air Force component for Special Operations Command Europe. Its squadrons are the 7th SOS, which flies the MC-130H Combat Talon II; the 21st SOS, equipped with the MH-53J Pave Low; and the 67th SOS, with the HC-130N/P Combat Shadow and the 321st Special Tactics Squadron.

353rd Special Operations Group
Residing at Kadena Air Base, Japan, is the Air Force component for Special Operations Command Pacific. The squadrons are the 1st SOS, which flies the MC-130E Combat Talon I; the 17th SOS, with the MC-130N/P Combat Shadow; and the 31st SOS at Osan Air Base, Korea, which flies the MH-53J Pave Low III helicopter.

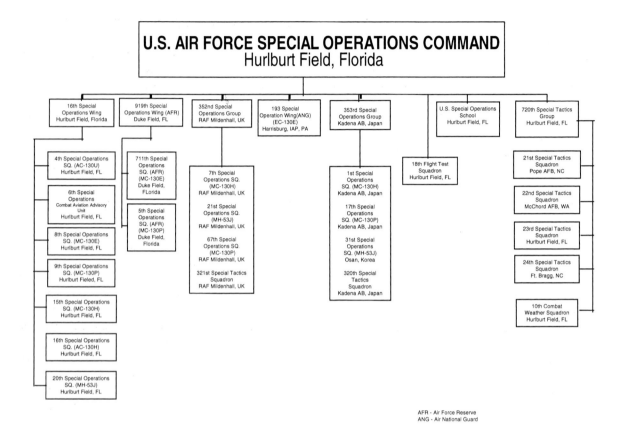

U.S. AIR FORCE SPECIAL OPERATIONS COMMAND
Hurlburt Field, Florida

- 16th Special Operations Wing, Hurlburt Field, Florida
  - 4th Special Operations SQ. (AC-130U), Hurlburt Field, FL
  - 6th Special Operations Combat Aviation Advisory Unit, Hurlburt Field, FL
  - 8th Special Operations SQ. (MC-130E), Hurlburt Field, FL
  - 9th Special Operations SQ. (MC-130P), Hurlburt Fieled, FL
  - 15th Special Operations SQ. (MC-130H), Hurlburt Field, FL
  - 16th Special Operations SQ. (AC-130H), Hurlburt Field, FL
  - 20th Special Operations SQ. (MH-53J), Hurlburt Field, FL
- 919th Special Operations Wing (AFR), Duke Field, FL
  - 711th Special Operations SQ. (AFR) (MC-130E), Duke Field, FLorida
  - 5th Special Operations SQ. (AFR) (MC-130P), Duke Field, Florida
- 352nd Special Operations Group, RAF Mildenhall, UK
  - 7th Special Operations SQ. (MC-130H), RAF Mildenhall, UK
  - 21st Special Operations SQ. (MH-53J), RAF Mildenhall, UK
  - 67th Special Operations SQ. (MC-130P), RAF Mildenhall, UK
  - 321st Special Tactics Squadron, RAF Mildenhall, UK
- 193 Special Operation Wing(ANG) (EC-130E), Harrisburg, IAP, PA
- 353rd Special Operations Group, Kadena AB, Japan
  - 1st Special Operations SQ. (MC-130H), Kadena AB, Japan
  - 17th Special Operations SQ. (MC-130P), Kadena AB, Japan
  - 31st Special Operations SQ. (MH-53J), Osan, Korea
  - 320th Special Tactics Squadron, Kadena AB, Japan
- U.S. Special Operations School, Hurlburt Field, FL
  - 18th Flight Test Squadron, Hurlburt Field, FL
- 720th Special Tactics Group, Hurlburt Field, FL
  - 21st Special Tactics Squadron, Pope AFB, NC
  - 22nd Special Tactics Squadron, McChord AFB, WA
  - 23rd Special Tactics Squadron, Hurlburt Field, FL
  - 24th Special Tactics Squadron, Ft. Bragg, NC
  - 10th Combat Weather Squadron, Hurlburt Field, FL

AFR - Air Force Reserve
ANG - Air National Guard

720th Special Tactics Group

Headquartered at Hurlburt Field, the 720th Special Tactics Group has units in the United States, Europe, and the Pacific. The group has special operations combat control teams and pararescue forces. Their missions include air traffic control for establishing air assault landing zones, close air support for strike aircraft and Spectre gunship missions, establishing casualty collection stations, and providing trauma care for injured personnel.

Its squadrons include the 21st STS at Pope Air Force Base, North Carolina; 22nd STS at McChord Air Force Base, Washington; 23rd STS at Hurlburt Field; the 24th STS located at Fort Bragg, North Carolina; and the 10th Combat Weather Squadron at Hurlburt Field.

U.S. Air Force Special Operations School

Reporting directly to AFSOC and at Hurlburt Field, the school provides special operations-related education to Department of Defense personnel, government agencies, and allied nations. More than 7,000 students attend the school each year.

Activated in April 1967, the USAF Special Air Warfare School was located at Eglin Air Force Base. In 1968 it was redesignated the USAF Special Operation School. It was in 1987 when the school, then under the command of the 23rd Air Force, was assigned to the U.S. Special Operations Command (USSOCOM) at MacDill Air Force Base, Tampa, Florida. On 22 May 1990 the school became a direct report of the newly established Air Force Special Operation Command (AFSOC) at Hurlburt Field.

The fundamental principle of the school is the belief that the key to success in special operations is the human element. Curriculum enhances the mission readiness and force survivability. Subjects covered in its 18 courses include introduction to special operations, regional affairs, cross-cultural communications, antiterrorism awareness, revolutionary warfare, joint psychological operations, joint special operations planning, joint aviation's foreign internal defense, and other classified areas. In fact, out of the 18 courses, 7 are rated "Secret" and another 6 receive the higher rating of "Top Secret."

18th Flight Test Squadron

With headquarters at Hurlburt Field, the 18th Flight Test provides expertise to improve the capabilities of special operations forces worldwide. The center conducts operational and maintenance suitability tests and evaluations for equipment, concepts, tactics, and procedures for employment of special operations forces. Many of these tests are joint command and joint service projects.

Air Reserve Components

AFSOC gains two Air Reserve Component units when the organizations are mobilized.

193rd Special Operations Group (Air National Guard)

Residing at Harrisburg International Airport, Pennsylvania, the 193rd is solely responsible for AFSOC's mission for providing airborne radio and television broadcasts. Flying the uniquely configured EC-130E Commando Solo aircraft, the unit can be deployed for PSYWAR operations during wartime or mobilized for humanitarian efforts in peacetime. Operating six of the Commando Solo aircraft, the 193rd can be deployed on a moment's notice around the globe. Anytime, anywhere.

919th Special Operations Wing (Air Force Reserve)

The 919th Special Operations Wing is located at Duke Field, Florida, whose 711th SOS—which once flew the AC-130A gunships—have been transitioned over to the MC-130E Combat Talon I. The squadron trains in the deployment of special operation forces or mission-critical equipment, day or night, at low levels into denied or hostile areas of operations. The 5th SOS flies the HC-130N/P Combat Shadow tanker. This unit flies clandestine missions into sensitive territories to provide air refueling for special operations aircraft. Secondary missions include air dropping special operation teams and other equipment as needed.

Chapter 3

New Missions

From early August 1990 to late February 1991, AFSOC participated in Operations Desert Shield and Desert Storm, the protection of Saudi Arabia, and liberation of Kuwait.

It was the Green Hornets Pave Lows of the 20th Special Operations Squadron that began the war in the Gulf. In October 1990, U.S. Commander in Chief Central Command (USCINCCENT) General Norman H. Schwarzkopf had studied the multitude of maps, aerial and satellite imagery, and intelligence reports and pondered his next plan of action. It was the last week of the month when Colonel Gary Gray of the 20th SOS met with the general. Col. Gray briefed Gen. Schwarzkopf on a plan called "Eager Anvil."

This plan intended for a flight of four MH-53 Pave Lows and an assault force of Army AH-64 Apache attack helicopters to execute the mission. The Pave Lows were equipped with FLIR, terrain avoidance radar, GPS, and other sophisticated electronics and navigational aids. They would cross into Iraq, leading the Apaches through the dark and over the featureless desert terrain to the target areas. Once on site the Army pilots in their Apaches would "take out" two enemy radar installations, simultaneously, with AGM-114 Hellfire laser-guided missiles. With these radar sites destroyed, a corridor opened for U.S. and Coalition aircraft to begin the air campaign.

So critical was this operation to the commencement of Desert Storm that Gen. Schwarzkopf asked

Col. Gray, "Colonel, are you going to guarantee me 100 percent success on this mission?" Col. Gray looked at the general and answered, "Yes, sir." The USCINCCENT replied, "Then you get to start the war."

Lieutenant Colonel Richard L. Comer was a little taken aback over Col. Gray's commitment. Comer vowed that the mission would have to be perfect; he did not intend to make his boss a liar. He later commented, "This was the best joint helicopter flying operation I've ever seen." The Apaches were designed to shoot and destroy targets, and the Pave Lows were designed to get the AH-64s to the targets; it was a perfect match. The designation for the mission was Task Force Normandy. There were two formations of two MH-53Js and two AH-64s. One group was assigned to the eastern site, the other to the westernmost installation.

AT 0212 TF Normandy crossed the border and entered Iraq. All of the training that the 20th had under their belts was now paying off. The helicopters sped through the pitch-black night flying no higher than 50 feet off the desert below. Relying on the Pave Lows' computers and sensors, the Green Hornets' pilots zigzagged around Nomad camps, down into wadis (a dry desert stream bed), flying NOE to stay under Iraqi radar. They staggered back and forth to avoid enemy observation posts.

The formations arrived on target, and at 0238 the sites were struck simultaneously by missiles. Within a span of four minutes, two Iraqi radar installations ceased to exist. The air campaign had begun. Active-duty AFRES and ANG components of AFSOC were deployed to Saudi Arabia and Turkey: the 1st SOW with its AC-130s, HC-130s, MC-130s, MH-53s, and MH-60s; the 193rd SOG with its EC-130s; and the 919th SOG, with its AC-130s and HH-3s all

The Special Tactics Team (STT) are a combination of Combat Controllers and Pararescuemen. The SST is the ground element of AFSOC, capable of being the "eyes and ears" of a theater commander. Here members of the 23rd Special Tactics Squadron are armed with the Colt M4 carbine.

AFSOC aircrews are at home in the darkness. It was the night capability and special navigational characteristics of the Pave Low that gave them the honor of starting the war in the Gulf. Using their advanced avionics and terrain avoidance radar, helicopters of the 20th SOS lead the way for U.S. Army AH-64 Apache helicopters into Iraq. Once on target the Apaches let loose the Hellfire missiles, destroying an Iraqi radar station, thus creating a corridor for coalition aircraft to commence the Air War. *AFSOC*

deployed south of Kuwait. The 39th SOW deployed north of Iraq with its HC-130s, MC-130s, and MH-53s. Special tactics personnel operated throughout the theater on multiple combat control and combat rescue missions.

Air Force Special Operation Command combat control teams were responsible for all air traffic control in the Persian Gulf theater of operation. In addition to this, other missions performed were direct-action missions, combat search and rescue, infiltration, exfiltration, air base ground defense, air interdiction, special reconnaissance, close air support, psychological operations, and helicopter air refueling.

A subdued patch of the Air Force Special Operations Command.

Post–Gulf War Events

Following the Gulf War, aircraft and personnel of the U.S. Air Force Special Operations Command stood alert for personnel recovery and various other missions. In April 1991, Operation PROVIDE COMFORT provided humanitarian assistance in northern Iraq to Kurdish refugees after a revolt against the Iraqi government failed and more than a million Kurds fled into the mountains along the Turkey and Iranian borders. Additionally, Operation Southern Watch monitored the area of southern Iraq to ensure no incursion of Iraqi troops below the 32nd parallel. In July 1992, AFSOC units began participation in NATO Implementation Force (IFOR) operations in Bosnia. Operation Provide Promise gave humanitarian relief. During this operation more than 15 tons of MREs (meals ready to eat) were air-dropped. Operation Deny Flight enforced the no-fly zone and provided close air support to United Nations ground troops. In December 1992, AFSOC special tactics and intelligence personnel supported Operation Restore Hope in Somalia. In the spring of 1993, under Operation Continue Hope, humanitarian relief operations were secured with the help of AC-130H Spectre gunships.

The number of deployments following Operation Desert Storm were only exceeded by the number of organizational modifications. The more significant ones included the 353rd SOW relocation under Operation Firey Vigil from Clark Air Base, Republic of Philippines, to Kadena Air Base, Japan, in June 1991 due to the volcanic eruption of Mount Pinatubo. The unit was supported by temporary duty personnel under Operation Scimatar Sweep for more than a year.

In January 1992, the 39th SOW relocated from Rhein-Main Air Base, Germany, to Royal Air Force Alconbury, United Kingdom, and later that year was inactivated and its personnel and equipment were reconstituted as the 352nd SOW. In December 1992, both overseas wings were redesignated as groups. During the summer of 1993 it was announced that the 352nd SOG would be moving again, this time to RAF Mildenhall.

More reorganization occurred on Hurlburt Field. The 1720th STGP became the 720th STG in March 1992. Ownership of Hurlburt Field was transferred from AMC to AFSOC in October 1992. This was followed by the merger of the 834th ABW into the 1st SOW, which assumed host unit responsibilities. A year later, the 1st SOW became the 16th SOW in a move to preserve Air Force heritage.

This PJ walks point, armed with an HK MP5 9-millimeter submachine-gun, the ever watchful eyes of an STT team member providing cover for the team. Note the personal radio AN/PRC 126.

Mission Criteria

Looking back on the special operations executed during Operation Urgent Fury in Grenada, special operation missions were hurriedly thrown together, with intelligence and parameters changing minute by minute. This resulted in the loss of life to several special operations troops. Grenada was an operation where all the forces wanted a piece of the pie, and consequently missions that might have been better suited to one force were tasked to another. It became a concern in the special operations community: They needed better mission assignments.

This issue was punctuated with the loss of four U.S. Navy SEALs at Paitilla Airport during Operation Just Cause in Panama. What started out as a small team of SEALs handling the attack expanded to such a large force, it grew out of the scope of normal mission profiles. It was common knowledge that you do not take down airfields with large groups of SEALs; you do it with U.S. Army Rangers. No longer just a concern, it was evident that clearly defined mission parameters needed to be established in the deployment of these highly trained, not easily replaced, special operations forces.

For the Air Commandos their mission parameters would fall under five mission criteria. These criteria would be carefully reviewed and applied prior to the planning and execution of operations requiring special operation forces. These guidelines would help SOF commanders and their staffs to objectively evaluate missions and give a clear set of standards to determine the feasibility and utility of AFSOC resources. They would also ensure these resources were used intelligently, allowing them to perform purposeful operations that would thereby contribute to the overall campaign.

These five criteria would be applied across the scope of military operations. First, the nature of the operations should be an appropriate special operation. During armed conflict SOF units should not be expected to carry out tasks that other units regularly train for, tasks that do not use the unique skills of SOF troops. Second, special operations must support the planned theater campaign. The commander-in-chief (CINC) establishes the command strategy and the special operations forces need to understand the CINC's priorities and goals, thus assuring that their units have the appropriate training and experience to support those strategies. Operations that do not support this strategy are to be avoided.

Third, special operation missions should be operationally feasible. Special operation forces cannot afford to waste resources on missions beyond their capability, as learned at Paitilla Airport. This does not suggest that special operations forces are not prepared to take on difficult tasks; it does mean that commanders must set realistic goals and understand limitations of certain operations. The fourth criteria requires available resources to actually execute the special operation mission. There are many parameters that are critical for the success of any special operation, including support in the manner of CAS, air refueling, ECM, diversions, and so on. In some cases other ongoing operations in a particular theater may preclude the use of SOF due to the unavailability of support assets. Finally, and perhaps the most critical, the expected outcome of any special operation must be worth the risk. Operations should not be conducted simply because the capabilities exist.

Chapter 4

Special Operations Aircraft

The backbone of the Special Operation Wings is the venerable Lockheed C-130s. With more than 40 years under its wings, the Hercules has more than lived up to its name. Its origins date back to the mid-fifties when the Air Force was looking for a turboprop transport to be used by the Military Airlift Transport Service (MATS), later known as Military Airlift Command (MAC) and the Tactical Air Command (TAC). The first production C-130, often called the "Herky-Bird," made its first flight on 7 April 1955. The initial deployment went to the Tactical Air Command in December 1956. The Hercules set an entirely new standard in tactical airlift. Through the years the C-130 has been in service in more than 20 countries and has evolved into many variants, four of which are important to special operations.

Tracing its heritage back to Vietnam, "Puff the Magic Dragon," "Spooky," "Stinger," and finally the moniker that stayed, the "Spectre," were names that brought fear into the hearts of the enemy forces and, more often than can be covered here, the relief and accolades of U.S. troops, both Special Forces and conventional. From its origin of the AC-47 with multiple miniguns through today, the gunship has evolved into a sophisticated, highly technical aircraft capable of turning the night sky into death. During Operation Restore Democracy in Haiti, Lieutenant Colonel Tim Schaffer of the 4th Special Operations Squadron reported that AFOSC put the Spectres on station even though there was no hostile activity. "It gave the troops on the ground peace of mind to hear the drone of those engines overhead, just in case."

AC-130U Spectre Gunship

The newest of the Spectre gunships and the current "flagship" of the Air Commando skies is the AC-130U. At a value of $72 million, this new Spectre was built with special operations in mind. Its primary mission is to deliver precision firepower in support of close air support for special operations and conventional ground forces. Close air support (CAS) is defined as air action against hostile targets that are in close proximity to friendly forces and require detailed integration of each air mission with the fire and movement of those forces. The Spectre can provide accurate fire support with limited collateral damage and can remain on station for extended periods of time. These activities are primarily performed in the cloak of darkness.

The business end of the gunship is found in three weapon systems. As you enter the AC-130U by way of the front crew hatch and turn to your right you'll find the first weapon system, the GAU-12/U 25-millimeter Gatling cannon, which is fully traversable and is also capable of firing 1,800 rounds per minute from altitudes of up to 12,000 feet. The 25-millimeter weapon system automatically ejects the spent brass into a holding area where it is emptied

The Fulton Surface-to-Air Recovery (STAR) apparatus fitted to an MC-130E Combat Talon I of the 8th SOS. Though no longer used, it is worth noting. This device, known as "Skyhook," allowed the extraction of special operations personnel. Personnel or equipment up to 500 pounds could be attached to a nylon line hoisted aloft by a balloon. As the Combat Talon approached, the yoke arms or "whiskers" on the front of the aircraft extended, enabling it to snag the line. The balloon breaks away and the line feeds into an attached power winch in the rear of the aircraft. The individual or cargo was then reeled into the aircraft via the rear ramp door.

The current pride of AFSOC, the AC-130U Spectre, has a crew of 13. This particular aircraft is in operations with the 4th Special Operations Squadron at Hurlburt Field, Florida.

out at a later time. There is no longer a need for the crew to shovel out the shell casings after a mission. This feature provides a safer environment for the crew as they will not trip over loose 25-millimeter shells on the fuselage floor. Munitions available for the GAU-12 include the PGU-25 and PGU-38 high-explosive incendiary (HEI) and PGU-23 target practice (TP) round. The PGU-25 and PGU-38 HEI are effective against exposed personnel and light materials with both fragmentation and incendiary effects. The PGU-23 TP is primarily used for target practice, although it does provide some penetration capability. The TP round is most effective when mixed with HEI to provide an impact signature.

Two holdovers from the A and H model gunships are the 40-millimeter Bofors guns and the 105-millimeter Howitzer cannon—both battle-tested weapons. The 40-millimeter Bofors gun has been associated with the gunships since 1969. Once used on naval vessels as anti-aircraft guns, the weapons were stripped down from pedestal mounts and placed in the AC-130s. The 40-millimeter Bofors is mounted in the port side of the AC-130U with the ammunition stored in a special rack on the starboard wall of the fuselage, behind the gun.

Ammunition for the 40-millimeter Bofors includes a variety of projectiles. The primary ordnance is the PGU-9B/B and PGU-9C/B High

Explosive Incendiary (HEI) Zirconium liner cartridges. Other cartridges include the PGU-9B HEI-P Misch metal liner, the MK-2 series HE-P and HEI-P cartridges (primarily used for training), and the M81 series Armor Piercing (AP) projectile, some of which contain 12-second-burn-time tracer elements (approximately 10,000 feet). The PGU-9B/B and PGU-9C/B HEI rounds are very effective against personnel, light vehicles, and as an incendiary for open flammables. The PRU-9B is a little less effective against the same target, as it contains less HE filler, resulting in a less effective fragmentation. The 40-millimeter is preferred for CAS in "danger close" support to friendly forces due to its small fragmentation pattern.

The other veteran on board, just aft of the Bofors, is the M102, 105-millimeter Howitzer cannon. This weapon was derived from the U.S. Army field artillery M1A1 Howitzer. It has been modified to fire from an aircraft and is placed in a special mounting and positioned in the port side of the gunship. The M102 fires both the M1, 32.5-pound high explosive (HE), and the M60, 34.2-pound white phosphorous (WP) projectile at a range of 11,500 meters. The fuses for the HE rounds are super-quick M557, selectable to point detonation or a 0.05 second time delay, the hard-end FMU-153B with point detonation or 0.004 to 0.009 second delay; and the M732 proximity fuse, which detonates approximately 7 meters above the ground or point detonation if not set for delay. The M1 HE projectiles with fast-fuse point detonation are effective against personnel and light vehicles. While the HE round with fuse delay is effective against light structures and personnel under heavy cover or foliage, the HE FMU-153B would be used for hardened target penetration capability. The M60 WP round, used only with the M557 fuse, is an effective smoke round with limited incendiary effect.

Unlike higher-speed fixed-wing aircraft (i.e., "fast movers"), which must have qualified forward air controllers (FAC) for ordnance delivery in close position to friendly forces, the AC-130U can be controlled by

An up-close-and-personal view of the 25-millimeter chain cannon. An upgrade from the 20-millimeter gun, this new 25-millimeter is traversable, and the crew no longer has to shovel spent brass after a fire mission. The unit will automatically dispose of the cartridges for later removal. No more tripping on shell casings.

fire support officers, team leaders, or self-FAC. This unique capability makes the gunship user-friendly for the operators on the ground, but requires a high degree of flexibility on the part of its crew.

These fire control officers are located onboard the gunship in the Battle Management Center or BMC. Here they operate the state-of-the-art sensors, navigation, and fire control systems in a work area protected by a composite armor of silicon carbide and Spectra fiber. The BMC, coupled with the trained eyes and skilled hands of its officers, enable the crew to deliver the Spectre's firepower or area saturation with surgical precision. This is accomplished even in adverse weather conditions and total darkness.

The assortment of sensors fitted in this modern gunship consist of an All Light Level Television (ALLTV) system, a laser illuminator assembly (LIA), and an infrared detection set. A multimode radar furnishes exceptionally long-range target direction and identification. This radar is also able to track 40-millimeter and 105-millimeter projectiles and

Aft weapons array shows the 40-millimeter Bofors and the 105-millimeter Howitzer cannon. Both weapon systems have been upgraded with improved electronics that allow the gunners to fire on two separate targets at the same time.

return pinpoint impact locations to the crew for subsequent target adjustment.

The fire control systems offer a Dual Target Attack capability. Engaging two different sensors and using both weapons, the 40-millimeter Bofors canon and 105-millimeter Howitzer have been updated with improved electronics that allow simultaneous aiming at two separate targets by the gunnery crew. As long as the two targets are within a mile of each other, the gunship can divide its fire with devastating accuracy. No other air-to-ground attack platform in the world offers this capability.

The new AC-130U is fully pressurized, allowing greater speeds, increased range, and additional crew comfort due to its ability to fly above, rather than through, adverse weather. Navigational features include inertial navigation systems (INS) and the GPS. The U-model gunship is capable of operation in adverse weather, in poor visibility using the APQ180 strike radar. The radar will track fixed or moving targets or beacon offsets.

Defensive systems include a countermeasures dispensing system that releases chaff and flares to counter radar and infrared-guided anti-aircraft missiles. To shield the aircraft's heat signature from the engines, the AC-130U has infrared heat shields mounted underneath the engines to dispense and hide the engine's heat source from hostile anti-aircraft missiles. Plans are in place to equip AFSOC aircraft with counter-IR devices with the introduction of the Directional Infrared Countermeasures system, or DIRCM. DIRCM fires a laser at incoming heat-seeking missiles, blinding their optics and ruining their ability to track the aircraft, causing it to miss.

While close air support is the Spectres' primary mission, additional tasks it may undertake include air interdiction, armed reconnaissance, airbase, perimeter, and point defense; land, water, and heliborne troop escort; drop, landing, and extraction zone support; forward air control; limited airborne command and control; and combat search and rescue support.

At the conclusion of extensive testing by the Air Force Flight Test Center, the U-model Spectre was delivered to AFSOC on 1 July 1994. Thirteen of these aircraft are now assigned to the 16th Special Operations Wing's 4th Special Operations Squadron.

AC-130U Specifications:

Contractor: Boeing, **powerplants:** four Allison T56-A15 turboprops; **thrust:** 4,910 equivalent shaft power; **wingspan:** 132 feet, 7 inches (40.4 meters); **length:** 97 feet, 9 inches (29.8 meters); **height:** 38 feet, 6 inches (11.7 meters); **speed:** 300 miles per hour (at sea level); **range:** approximately 2,200 nautical miles, unlimited with air refueling; **ceiling:** 30,000 feet; **maximum takeoff weight:** 155,000 pounds (peacetime), 175,000 pounds (wartime); **armament:** one GAU-12/U 25-millimeter General Electric Gatling gun (firing rate of 1,800 rounds per minute), one L-60 40-millimeter Bofors cannon (firing rate of 100 shots per minute), one M-102 105-millimeter cannon (firing rate of 6 to 10 rounds per minute.); **avionics:** Hughes APG-80 Fire Control Radar, Texas Instruments AN/AAQ-117 Forward Looking Infra-Red (FLIR) for 180 degree IR scanning, Gec-Marconi

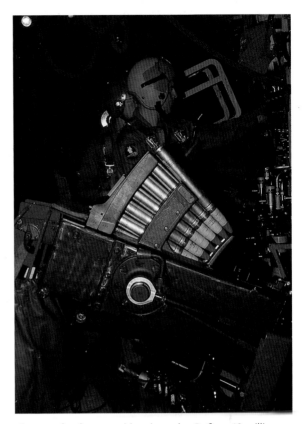

Gunners load ammunition into the Bofors 40-millimeter cannon. The 40-millimeter ammo comes in stacks of four per pack and can be continuously fed into the weapon as it fires.

All Active Low Light Level TeleVision (AALLLTV), INS/GPS navigation, ALQ-172 RF Electronic Countermeasures System, and ALR-69 Radar Warning Receiver; **crew:** 13 total—five officers (pilot, copilot, navigator, fire control officer, and electronic warfare officer) and eight enlisted (flight engineer, ALLTV operator, IR detection operator, four gunners, and loadmaster).

AC-130H Spectre Gunship

The predecessor to the U-model, the H-model Spectre gunship, armed with 20-, 40-, and 105-millimeter

The Fulton Surface-to-Air Recovery System

The Fulton Surface-to-Air Recovery System (STAR), also known as "Skyhook," allows the extraction of special operations personnel from the ground. The STAR device consists of two containers that can be air-dropped to Special Forces units operating in a covert operation. Upon opening the canisters the soldiers on the ground would find a balloon, which when inflated with the two accompanying helium bottles will measure 8 feet in diameter by 23 feet in length. Five hundred-foot nylon lines would be attached to the balloon. These lines are equipped with marker flags for daylight extractions and strobe lights for night operations.

The individual to be extracted would put on the insulated flight suit and harness found in one of the canisters. At this time he would be hooked up to the balloon's lines and then sit facing the oncoming plane as the balloon is released and heads skyward.

As the Combat Talon approached the recovery area the yoke arms or "whiskers" extend. These arms snag the line in a locking device. The balloon will break away and the line will feed into an attached hydraulic power winch in the rear of the aircraft. The individual will then be reeled into the ramp door.

Along with personnel, the STAR system could also recover up to 500 pounds of equipment or material if need be.

Truly a unique method of exfiltration, it was only the Talon crews of the 8th Special Operations Squadron that maintained proficiency with the STAR system. The Talons of the 8th SOS have trained and been prepared to launch, if requested, since the late sixties. In the 17 years of live extractions there was only one fatality. This accident, however, gave pause to the special operations community, and there was damage to the credibility of the system among some operators. As unequaled as the Fulton system was, there were major concerns—this, and the fact that the MH-53J Pave Lows, MH-60 Pave Hawks, and the MH47E Chinooks (of the 160th SOAR) have a capacity of long-range, air-refueling capabilities.

Lieutenant Colonel Bernard V. Moore, commander of the 8th SOS, commented on the STAR system: "Special operation forces no longer have a requirement for it [STAR], and our customers are not requesting it." With the decreased need and tightening budgets, AFSOC deactivated the system on 14 September 1997, after 30 years in the Air Commandos' inventory.

---

cannons, can deliver precision firepower in support of close air support missions. This includes alternate missions: air interdiction; armed reconnaissance; airbase, perimeter, and point defense; land, water, and heliborne troop escort; drop, landing, and extraction zone support; forward air control; limited airborne command and control; and CSAR support.

Heavily armed, the AC-130H incorporates side-firing weapons integrated with sophisticated sensor, navigation, and fire control systems to provide surgical firepower or area saturation during extended periods, primarily at night as well as in inclement weather.

Included in the sensor array you'll find low-light television (LLTV) and infrared (IR) sensors. The H-model is also equipped with radar and electronic devices that give the gunship a positive IFF (Identify Friend/Foe) to distinguish between supporting friendly ground forces and efficient delivery of ordnance on hostiles during all weather conditions.

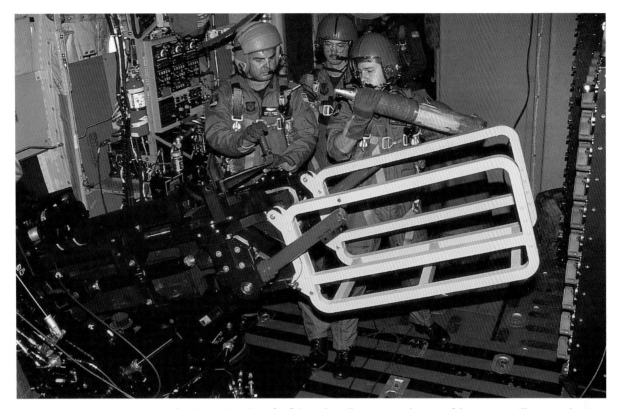

The Spectre's gun crew prepares the 105mm Howitzer for firing. The yellow cage at the rear of the cannon will protect the crew from recoil.

Navigation devices include an inertial navigation system and GPS.

During Operation Desert Storm, the Spectres provided air base defense and close air support for ground forces. While AFSOC aircraft and squadrons would play a primary role, it would not be without a high cost. AFSOC suffered its only loss of the war, an AC-130H of the 16th Special Operation Squadron—"Spirit 03" and a crew of 14. This was the single largest "air" loss during the Persian Gulf War. Once again, the men of AFSOC would live up to the heritage of the Air Commandos and make the ultimate sacrifice for their country and freedom.

Subsequently, the AC-130s were also used in Operation Continue Hope and United Shield in Somalia. In addition, Spectre gunships played a pivotal role in support of IFOR missions in Bosnia-Herzegovina. As NATO launched a three-day assault on Bosnian Serb targets, AC-130H gunships were tasked with targeting and destroying artillery and radar sites positioned around Sarajevo.

AC-130H Specifications:
Contractor: Lockheed; **powerplant:** four Allison turboprop engines T56-A15; **thrust:** 4,910 equivalent shaft power; **wingspan:** 132 feet, 7 inches (40.4 meters); **length:** 97 feet, 9 inches (29.8 meters); **height:** 38 feet, 6 inches (11.7 meters); **speed:** 300 miles per hour (at sea level); **range:** approximately 2,200 nautical miles, unlimited

In the belly of the aircraft is the Battle Management Center. Here the fire control officer, electronic warfare officers, and enlisted crew members will monitor ALLTV, thermal imagers, and surveillance and targeting devices. The fire control officer uses a joystick to pick out targets on the ground. This information is then passed on to the aircraft commander.

with air refueling; **ceiling:** 30,000 feet; **maximum takeoff weight:** 155,000 pounds (peacetime), 175,000 pounds (wartime); **armament:** two 20-millimeter Vulcan cannons with 3,000 rounds, one 40-millimeter Bofors cannon with 256 rounds, and one 105-millimeter Howitzer with 100 rounds; **crew:** 14 total, 5 officers (pilot, copilot, navigator, fire control officer, and electronic warfare [EW] officer) and 9 enlisted (flight engineer, LLTV operator, IR detection operator, 5 gunners, and a loadmaster).

MC-130E/H Combat Talon

The MC-130E Combat Talon I and the MC-130H

Combat Talon II are designed for long-range clandestine or covert delivery of special operations forces and equipment and to provide global, day, night, and adverse weather capability to air-drop and air-land personnel and equipment in support of U.S. and allied special operation forces.

Combat Talons are equipped with FLIR, terrain following/avoidance radars, and specialized aerial delivery equipment. Incorporated into the Talons are a fully integrated inertial navigation (IIN), GPS, and a high-speed aerial delivery system. These special systems are used to locate small drop zones and deliver personnel or equipment with greater accuracy and at

Banking to the left, Captain Charles Bruner of the 4th SOS lines up his AC-130U gunship. He views the target through a HUD unit and when ready, fires the weapons

higher speeds than possible with a "vanilla" C-130. Such an example is Army Special Forces (Green Berets) or U.S. Navy SEALs operating in a sensitive or hostile territory. Nine of the MC-130Es had been equipped with the Fulton Surface-to-Air Recovery (STAR) system.

MC-130E/H Combat Talons are able to penetrate hostile airspace at low altitudes to carry out these missions. Talon crews are specially trained in night and adverse weather operations. It is well known that instrument flight rules, or IFR, govern ordinary aircraft flying through clouds. The Talons use their own version of IFR called *infrared* flight rules,

which basically ignores all the rules and allows them to fly at high speeds at low levels in heavy ground fog or low cloud cover.

The MC-130H, Combat Talon II features highly automated controls and display that will reduce the crew size and work load. The flightdeck as well as the cargo areas are compatible with night vision goggles. The integrated control and display subsystem combines basic aircraft flight, tactical, and mission sensor data into a comprehensive set of display formats that assist each operator as he performs the tasks.

The pilot and co-pilot display formats include basic flight instrumentation and situational data.

A closer look at the altitude indicator on the instrument cluster indicates that the SPECTRE is in a pylon turn. The AC-130U performs a banking maneuver, so its weapons point toward the designated targets.

The display formats are available with symbology alone or with symbology overlaid with sensor video. The navigator uses radar ground map displays, FLIR display, tabular missions management display, and equipment status information. The EW officer's displays are used for viewing the EW data and to supplement the navigators in certain critical mission phases.

During Operation Desert Storm, the MC-130E Combat Talon I played a vital role. One-third of all air drops in the first three weeks of the war were carried out by MC-130s. The primary role was that of psychological operation, as it air-dropped 11 BLU-82/B general-purpose bombs—a rather pedestrian name for a 15,000-pound bomb. Make no mistake, a 7 1/2-ton

bomb makes quite an impression. When they exploded, a British SAS team radioed back to headquarters that, ". . . the Yanks were using nukes. . . ." Along with the bomb runs, the Talons also flew multiple mission air-dropping leaflets. A secondary role was in the CSAR missions.

MC-130E/H Specifications:

Contractor: Lockheed; **powerplant:** four Allison turboprop engines T56-A15; **thrust:** 4,910 equivalent shaft power; **wingspan:** 132 feet, 7 inches (40.4 meters); **length:** MC-130E, 100 feet, 10 inches (30.7 meters); MC-130H, 99 feet, 9 inches (30.4 meters); **height:** 38 feet, 6 inches (11.7 meters); **speed:** 300

miles per hour (at sea level); **range:** approximately 3,110 nautical miles, unlimited with air refueling; **ceiling:** 30,000 feet; **maximum takeoff weight:** 155,000 pounds; **load:** MC-130E, 53 troops or 26 paratroops; MC-130H, 75 troops or 52 paratroops; **crew:** MC-130E, 9 total—5 officers (2 pilots, 2 navigators, and 1 EW officer) and 4 enlisted (1 flight engineer, 2 loadmasters, and 1 communications specialist); MC-130H, 7 total—4 officers (2 pilots, 1 navigator, and 1 EW officer) and 3 enlisted (1 flight engineer and 2 loadmasters).

MC-130P Combat Shadow

The Combat Shadow extends the range of special operations helicopters by providing air refueling. Operations are conducted primarily in formation, at night, at low-level to reduce the probability of visual acquisition and intercept by airborne threats. This is carried out in clandestine, low-level missions into politically sensitive or hostile territory. The Shadow is a visual flight rule (VFR) aircraft and would only be used when the pilots can see the ground, although penetrations are often aided by radar. The MC-130P may fly in a multiship or single-ship mission to reduce detection.

The secondary mission of the Combat Shadow includes the delivery of special operation forces. Small teams, assorted gear, equipment, Zodiacs, and combat rubber raiding craft (CRRC) are a few of the specialized items that are conveyed by the aircraft and its crew.

The Combat Shadow has a full IIN, GPS, and NVG-compatible lighting for the interior and exterior. This allows the crew to use NVG-compatible heads-up display (HUD) to fly the plane. It has a FLIR, missile, and radar warning receiver to alert the crew of threats. Countermeasure devices include chaff and flare dispensers. Communications have satellite and data burst technology. In addition, the MC-130P will have in-flight refueling capability as a receiver.

Originally designated the HC-130 N/P, Air Force special operation aircraft were redesignated in February

The "First Lady" of the 919th Special Operation Wing, this AC-130A makes its last appearance prior to being decommissioned and taking its place at the Air Force Armament Museum in Florida. She is one of the original Spectres. Shown here is a good view of the forward pod of a twin 20-millimeter chain cannon, along with the crest of the 919th SOW.

Here we see a later modification of the AC-130. While it retains its twin 20-millimeter Vulcan cannons similar to the A model, the H model has removed one of the Bofors 40-millimeter and added a 105-millimeter Howitzer cannon in its place. The AN/APQ-150 RADAR unit can be seen between the barrels.

1996 to correspond with all other M-series special operations aircraft.

MC-130Ps have been actively employed in special operations mission since the mid-1980s. These clandestine refuelers were deployed to Saudi Arabia to support Desert Storm in 1990. They provided the necessary air refueling of special operations forces helicopters. This was carried out in both coalition and hostile territory. Combat Shadows were also used in psychological operations and leaflet drops. One of these leaflets carried the following admonition to Iraqi troops:

Warning! This is only the beginning! This could have been a real bomb. We have no desire to harm innocent people, but Saddam is leading you to certain death and destruction. We want you to know the truth. Saddam is the cause. Yes, the Multi-National Forces have the ability to strike anywhere . . . and at anytime! Warning."

Such leaflets were responsible for hundreds of Iraqi troops surrendering without a shot being fired. During the course of the war, the 8th Special Operations Squadron and the 9th SOS dropped more than 17 million leaflets. Combat Shadows have also been employed as combat search and rescue as well as command and control aircraft.

MC-130P Specifications:

Contractor: Lockheed; **powerplant:** four Allison turboprop engines T56-A15; **thrust:** 4,910 equivalent shaft power; **wingspan:** 132 feet, 7 inches (40.4 meters); **length:** 97 feet, 9 inches (29.8 meters); **height:** 38 feet, 6 inches (11.7 meters); **speed:** 289 miles per hour (at sea level); **range:** approximately

An MC-130H Combat Talon II of the 15th SOS on the tarmac at Hurlburt Field. To keep the avionics cool while running on the ground, an air-conditioning unit is attached to the aircraft.

A Combat Talon prepares to lift off the tarmac at Hurlburt Field. Encased in that large nose is the AN/APQ-170 Multi Mode Radar (MMR). Directly beneath can be seen the forward looking infrared, or FLIR, allowing the Talon to penetrate hostile airspace. The E version is painted in the older camouflage patterns of green. The new color scheme is a matte gray. Soon all AFSOC aircraft, both fixed wing and rotary, will be the same color.

4,000 nautical miles, unlimited with air refueling; ceiling: 33,000 feet; **maximum takeoff weight:** 155,000 pounds (peacetime), 175,000 pounds (wartime); **crew:** eight total—four officers (pilot, copilot, primary navigator, and secondary navigator), and four enlisted (flight engineer, communications operator, and two loadmasters).

EC-130E Rivet Rider Commando Solo

The Commando Solo, formally known as the Volant Solo, is flown by the 193rd Special Operations Group. It is the only AFSOC asset that is an Air National Guard entity. It has seen action from Operation Urgent Fury in 1983 during the assault on Grenada, to Operation Just Cause in 1989 in Panama. It served as the "Voice of the Gulf" during Operation Desert Storm in 1991, convincing Iraqi soldiers to surrender; and also in Operation Uphold Democracy in 1994 as a broadcasting platform during the Haitian uprising.

As the name implies, the Commando Solo works alone. It is capable of conducting day and night overt or covert operations. The primary mission of the EC-130 is to conduct psychological operations, civil affairs broadcast missions, and electronic countermeasures. This is accomplished by using standard AM/FM radio, HF/shortwave, TV, and tactical military communications frequencies while loitering outside the lethal range of any weapons possessed by enemy forces. The crew of the Commando Solo will carry out its PSYWAR mission both day and night, operating at the maximum altitudes to achieve maximum possible transmission into the given area of operation. Typical mission parameters will find a single EC-130E circling the target audience, whether it be military or civilian.

The EC-130 is not only capable of jamming enemy signals and communications, but it is also effective in pinpointing any attempts to jam communication by the enemy. Once the source is located, this information is passed on to the appropriate chain, and the electronic threat can be neutralized. If the enemy signal is something other than just noise, an alternate option would allow the enemy force to continue

An MC-130P Combat Shadow. Note that this Shadow has had the STAR recovery arms removed from its nose. The MC-130P serves as an air refueler for AFSOC helicopters and can also be used as an insertion platform for STT teams. Note the silhouettes of the team toward the rear of the aircraft.

communicating and intercept their communications. Alternate missions include command and control, communications, countermeasures (C3CM), and occasionally intelligence gathering.

Overflowing with highly sophisticated electronics and mission-critical specialized modifications, the EC-130E incorporates enhanced navigation systems, self-protection equipment, secure fax machines, and computers. In addition to these devices, there are VCRs, cassettes, compact disks, and powerful transmitters that are capable of broadcasting color television on a multitude of worldwide standards, throughout the TV VHF/UHF ranges.

EC-130E Specifications:

Contractor: Lockheed; **powerplant:** four Allison turboprop engines T56-A15; **thrust:** 4,910 equivalent shaft power; **wingspan:** 132 feet, 7 inches (40.4 meters); **length:** 100 feet, 6 inches (30.9 meters); **height:** 38 feet, 6 inches (11.7 meters); **Speed:** 299 miles per hour (at sea level); **range:** Approximately 2,100 nautical miles (3,380 kilometers), unlimited with air refueling; **ceiling:** 20,000 feet; **maximum takeoff weight:** 155,000 pounds (70,455 kilograms); **crew:** 11 total—4 officers (pilot, copilot, navigator, mission control chief/electronic warfare officer) and 7 enlisted (flight engineer, loadmaster, and 5 mission crew).

The refueling hose of this Combat Shadow is tucked into the pod. Upon rendezvous with the hungry choppers, the hose and drogue unreels from the pod and streams along behind the aircraft, allowing them to hook up their probes and take on fuel.

The home office of the MC-130P, the flight deck. Here the pilot, copilot, and flight engineer carry out the mission of getting their cargo delivered. In this case it is an STT and a RAMZ drop.

MH-53J Pave Low III

The mission of the MH-53J is to carry out low-level, long-range, undetected ingress into denied or hostile areas. This is accomplished day or night, even under the worst weather conditions for infiltration, exfiltration, and resupply of special operations forces.

Like its forerunner, the Sikorsky HH-53 Jolly Green Giant of the Vietnam era, the MH-53J Pave Low III Enhanced is the main helicopter in service with the Air Force Special Operations Command.

Unlike its predecessor, it has been modified and augmented with state-of-the-art technology that the Jolly Green pilots would have killed for in their day.

The Pave Low is the largest and most powerful helicopter in the U.S. Air Force inventory and the most technologically advanced helicopter in the world. Equipped with forward-looking infrared, inertial GPS, Doppler navigation systems, a terrain-following/avoidance radar, an on-board computer, and integrated advanced avionics enable it to achieve precise, low-level, long-range penetration into denied areas, day or night, in adverse weather and over hazardous terrain without detection.

In the spring of 1999, AFSOC began modifying the MH-53J Pave Low with Interactive Defensive Avionics System/Multi-Mission Advanced Tactical Terminal (IDAS/MATT). This modification will provide the air crews with a heightened level of readiness and efficiency. The new designation for the Pave Low helicopters with this modification is the M model. This system is a color, multifunctional, night-vision–compatible, digital map screen. Located on the helicopter's instrument panel, the display gives the crew a more concise view of the battlefield and instant access to real time events. The helicopter's flight path, manmade obstacles such as power lines, and even hostile threats "over the horizon" are depicted in an easy-to-read manner.

The system receives its data from a satellite, directly into the computer. The signal is then decoded and the data is displayed in 3-D color imaging of the surrounding terrain, including contour lines and elevation bands. At the push of a button the crew can visualize a digital navigational course and bearing

As of this writing, women are not allowed in STTs, although they may be found in support functions as in the case of this major, a navigator on an MC-130P.

The Voice of the Air Commandos, the EC-130 Rivet Raider. Here a Commando Solo flies a training mission over the Three Mile Island nuclear facility in Pennsylvania. *AFSOC*

information, in addition to the map display. Designed to give crew members a priority in consolidating the variety of functions, extra detail was taken to provide the crew easy-to-control instrument panel functions while increasing the flow of information efficiently.

All of this high technology results in what the Air Force calls the "crew concept"; the pilot of the MH-53J gets assistance from the co-pilot and flight engineer. These three individuals are crammed into the flight deck, smaller than an average-sized closet. Each one has his responsibility and a section of the controls to manage. Together, they make the Pave Low maneuver in such a way that staggers the imagination, and sometimes the stomach.

Offering protection to the crew is armor plating as well as an assortment of weapon systems. Just aft of the flight deck are two 7.62-millimeter miniguns, and at the rear of the helicopter on the exit ramp is a .50-caliber machine gun. While the mission of the Pave Low is primarily an INFIL/EXFIL platform, with all the previously mentioned weapons, it also serves as a helicopter gunship. With a combination of armor, weaponry, and maneuverability, the crew is pretty well covered.

An STT member fast ropes from an MH-60 Pave Hawk. STT troops are trained in the fast rope insertion system (FRIS). While it can be used as low as 10 feet, the normal range is between 30 and 120 feet. Using the FRIS, an entire STT can egress from a hovering helicopter and be on the ground in a matter of seconds, ready to execute their mission. An alternate method of insertion and extraction is the rope ladder. Master Sergeant Rick Weaver of the Pararescue School at Kirtland Air Force Base explains, "The rope ladder is primarily used in an over-the-water environment." There are times, when due to uneven terrain or no HLZ, it may be deployed over the ground.

During Operation Desert Storm, an AFSOC MH-53J guided the U.S. Army AH-64 Apaches to their targets deep inside Iraq. Flying over hundreds of miles of featureless desert, the Air Commandos led the lethal sortie directly to two Iraqi early-warning radar stations. Here the Apaches destroyed the Iraqi ground targets using Hellfire missiles. This opened a corridor for U.S. and coalition forces to begin the air war.

In addition to providing infiltration, exfiltration, and resupply of special operation forces, the Pave Lows provided CSAR coverage for coalition air forces in Iraq, Saudi Arabia, Kuwait, Turkey, and the Persian Gulf. An MH-53J, call sign Moccasin 5, made the first successful combat recovery of a downed pilot in Desert Storm. At the conclusion of the war, the Pave Lows would see service in Northern Iraq to support Operation Provide Comfort, assisting the Kurds, and later on with IFOR operations in Bosnia.

MH-53J Specifications:

Contractor: Sikorsky Aircraft Corporation; **power-plant:** two General Electric T64-GE/100 engines; **thrust:** 4,339 shaft horsepower per engine; **length:** 92 feet (27.88 meters); **height:** 25 feet (7.58 meters); **rotary diameter:** 72 feet (21.88 meters); **blades per hub:** six; **speed:** 195 miles per hour (312 kilometers per hour); **range:** 630 statute miles (548 nautical miles), unlimited with air refueling; **ceiling:** 16,000 feet (4,849 meters); **maximum takeoff weight:** 42,000 pounds (18,900 kilograms); **armament:** any combination of three 7.62-millimeter miniguns and .50-caliber machine guns; **payload:** 38 fully equipped combat troops, or 14 litters; its external cargo hook is also capable of 20,000 pounds (9,000 kilograms); **crew:** six total—two officers (pilots) and four enlisted (two flight engineers and two aerial gunners).

CV-22 "Osprey"

The Osprey is a tilt-rotor vertical lift aircraft, which means it takes off like a helicopter and flies like a conventional airplane. There is nothing conven-

An MH-53J Pave Low III E helicopter of the 20th SOS, call sign "Cowboy Zero-3," just dropped off an STT and prepares to take off and assume an orbit over the team. It will be on station to provide CAS when called on by the team on the ground.

55thSOS/MH-60G

In the fall of 1999, the 55th SOS, which flies the MH-60G Pave Hawk helicopter, was inactivated. After distinguished service in the AFSOC, the six MH-60 Pave Hawk helicopters were transferred to Air Combat Command. The transfer augments ACC aircraft in their role in conventional search and rescue.

The primary missions of the MH-60G, the Pave Hawk, were infiltration, exfiltration, and resupply of special operations forces. This is accomplished day, night, or in marginal weather conditions. Secondary missions included combat search and rescue (CSAR).

The twin-engine, medium-lift helicopter is fitted with an all-weather radar so the crew of the Pave Hawk is able to locate and avoid inclement weather. The automatic flight control system is used to stabilize the aircraft in typical flight altitudes. They also have instrumentation and engine and rotor blade anti-ice systems for all-weather operation.

Equipped with a retractable refueling probe, the MH-60G is capable of receiving inflight refueling to its internal auxiliary fuel tanks. This will extend its range from 445 statute miles to unlimited to carry out missions. The helicopter can carry 8 to 10 troops; these "operators" are capable of rapid loading and unloading through sliding doors aft of the cabin windows on either side of the aircraft. The nonretractable landing gear and tail wheel facilitate a short step to the LZ rather than a large hop intrinsic in the old "Hueys."

As a gunship or in a defense posture, the MH-60G is equipped with two 7.62-millimeter miniguns mounted in the cabin windows aft of the flight deck. It is also possible to mount two .50-caliber machine guns in the cabin doors. To further augment the weapons, there may be added an external stores support system (ESSS), which will allow the addition of 2.75-inch rocket pods, 20-millimeter cannon pods, or two .50-caliber machine guns. This makes the helicopter a formidable weapons platform in the AFSOC inventory and with the Special Forces troops it operates. It will be a welcome asset to the SAR capability of ACC.

Specifications:

Contractor: Sikorsky Aircraft Corporation; **powerplant**: two General Electric T700-GE-01C engines; **thrust**: 1,630 shaft horsepower per engine; **length**: 64 feet, 8 inches (17.1 meters); **height**: 16 feet, 8 inches (4.4 meters); **rotary diameter**: 53 feet, 7 inches (14.1 meters); **blades per hub**: four; **speed**: 184 miles per hour (294.4 kilometers per hour); **range**: 445 statute miles (504 nautical miles), unlimited with air refueling; **maximum takeoff weight**: 22,000 pounds (9,900 kilograms); **armament**: two 7.62-millimeter miniguns; **payload**: 8 to 10 troops, external load of 8,000 pounds (3,600 kilograms) on cargo hook; **crew**: four total. Two officers (pilots) and two enlisted (one flight engineer and one aerial gunner).

tional about the Osprey, however. Development of the V-22 program began in 1981 and was originally designed for the U.S. Marines, designated the MV-22. Planned for introduction into AFSOC forces in 2003, the CV-22 is a special operations variant of the MV-22.

The CV-22 will differ from the MV-22 with the addition of a third seat in the cockpit for a flight

engineer and will be fitted with a refueling probe to facilitate midair refueling. Additionally, the AFSOC version of the Osprey will have the modern suite of electronics, like those installed in other AFSOC aircraft, items such as a multimode terrain-avoidance and terrain-following radar. To deal with the nature of special operations, it will have enhanced EW equipment for increased battlefield

A newly upgraded MH-53M Pave Low, modified with the Interactive Defense Avionics System/Multimission Advance Tactical Terminal (IDAS/MATT). Although regularly modified and upgraded, these helicopters are older than most of the crews flying them. For example, this helicopter was used on the Son Tay raid into North Vietnam.

awareness, with more than 2.5 times the volume of flares and chaff, radar-jamming gear, and improved integration of defensive countermeasures. For CSAR it will have an internally mounted rescue hoist and a crew door located on the starboard side of the aircraft. Another significant difference between the AFSOC and Marine version will be the amount of fuel it will carry. The CV-22 carries approximately twice the amount of fuel of the MV-22 variant.

The $49.7 million CV-22 is intended to eventually replace AFSOC's entire fleet of MH-53 Pave Low and MH-60G Pave Hawk helicopters. There are even suggestions that it will phase out some of the MC-130E Combat Talon I and MC-130P/N Combat Shadows. Once deployed it is expected that 50 CV-22 Ospreys will replace up to 89 current AFSOC aircraft. The mission of the CV-22 will be to infil/exfil and resupply special operations forces in denied or enemy area in total darkness in all weather.

CV-22 Specifications:

Contractor: Bell Helicopter Textron/Boeing Helicopter; **powerplant:** Two Allison T406-AD-400 engines; **thrust:** 6,150 shaft horsepower per engine (maximum); **wingspan:** 45 feet, 9 inches (13.9 meters); **length:** 57 feet, 33 inches (17.48meters); **height:** 21 feet, 9.5 inches (6.63 meters); **rotary diameter:** 38 feet (14.1 meters); **width, rotors turning:** 83 feet, 33 inches (25.55 meters); **blades per hub:** three; **speed:** 510 miles per hour (275 kilometers per hour); **range:** 515 nautical miles, unlimited with air refueling; **maximum takeoff weight:** vertical, 47,500 pounds (21,546 kilograms); short running, 55,000 pounds (24,948 kilograms); **armament:** 2 7.62-millimeter miniguns; **payload:** 24 cargo troops, 12 litters or 20,000 pounds internal, external load of 10,000 pounds (4,536 kilograms) on single cargo hook, 15,000 pounds (9,221 kilograms) dual cargo hook; **crew:** 4 total, 2 pilots and 2 flight engineers.

In spring 1999, AFSOC began upgrading the Pave Low with IDAS/MATT. IDAS improves combat survivability, provides flexible integrated EW, and incorporates existing defensive systems and the cockpit-mounted digital map system (DMS). MATT is a multiservice program that takes a real-time over-the-horizon threat and intelligence data and real-time Electronic Order of Battle alerts and updates, and integrates them onto cockpit avionics displays. The heart of IDAS/MATT is the DMS. DMS adds cockpit-mounted Color Multi-Function Displays, NVG compatible lighting, and multifunction display capability for existing pilot video monitors. The displays help guide crews through mountainous terrain, show digital maps in various scales depicting the aircraft's course, and provide a visual display of threat and intelligence data. Fully modified Pave Low helicopters are now designated M models.

Although it is a large helicopter capable of transporting 38 combat troops, the crew of the Pave Low works in a very small area. This view shows the two side gunners with the flight deck just beyond them. Here the pilot, copilot, and flight engineer work together as a team in an area smaller than some walk-in closets.

One of the Pave Low's gunners readies the M-2 .50-caliber machine gun. With a shell more than 5 inches long, it is a formidable weapon against troops, bunkers, and soft-skinned vehicles such as armored personnel carriers.

The stinger in the hornet's tail. Located on the rear cargo ramp of the Pave Low, a gunner mans the "Ma-Deuce" or the M-2 .50-caliber machine gun. If you note the horizon in this photo, you'll get an idea of how maneuverable the Pave Low can be despite its massive size.

The starboard gunner of the Pave Low engages the minigun. This 7.62-millimeter minigun is capable of putting thousands of rounds per minute on target.

This bank of radios, referred to as the "pizza rack," is not for tuning in the DJ at the local radio station. These radios provide the crew the necessary communications with forces on the ground, other aircraft, and AWACS.

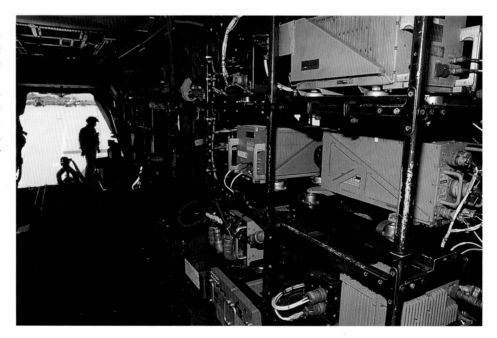

Unconventional warfare calls for an unconventional aircraft, the CV-22 tilt-rotor. Some question whether this is an airplane or a helicopter, while others ask if it is a tactical aircraft or political aircraft. The Osprey program has gone through more revivals than a TV evangelist. With modifications on the MV-22 platform, AFSOC intends the aircraft to succeed the aging helicopters and some MC-130s. The CV-22 is planned to be in service with AFSOC by 2003. *U.S. Navy/Bell Boeing*

You will find no greater ride in AFSOC to get your heart pounding than on a Pave Low. The pilots of the 20th SOS can thread a needle with this 92-foot helicopter. One Green Hornet pilot confesses that flying at tree-top level, in the black of night with NODs, although dangerous, is ". . . kind of a cool thing!"

As MV-22 was originally developed for the U.S. Marines, it has several limitations for current SOF missions. One noticeable concern: There is no land-based vehicle in the current SOF inventory able to fit inside it, including the RATT or the FAV. This issue is being addressed in the design of a new "light strike vehicle" capable of being deployed from the Osprey. *U.S. Navy/Bell Boeing*

Chapter 5

Special Tactics Squadrons

The U.S. Army has the Rangers and the Special Forces (the Green Berets). In the U.S. Navy the special operators are the SEALs. Rounding out the full force of the U.S. special operations forces on the ground are the men of the U.S. Air Force Special Operation Command Special Tactics Squadrons. A combination of CCT and PJs is referred to as a Special Tactics Team, or STT. The STT is an integral part of the U.S. Special Operations Command and its missions. STT members frequently operate with the U.S. Navy SEALs, U.S. Army Rangers, and U.S. Army Special Forces units in SR, CSAR, and DA (i.e., airfield seizure), to name just a few of their capabilities. Every member of the STS teams is a volunteer. These highly motivated, proficient STTs are capable of being deployed by sea, air, or land (sound familiar?) often weighed down with 100 to 150 pounds of equipment to execute their mission. These units will be found regularly on missions alongside the U.S. Army and U.S Navy SOF troops. Whether they fast-rope in with a company of Rangers, high-altitude low-opening (HALO) parachute in with a Special Forces "A-Team," or lock-out a submarine with a SEAL platoon, STS teams are qualified in these skills and add a lethal element to U.S. special operation forces.

Special Tactics Combat Control and Pararescue

Operating under the AFSOC, the Special Tactics Squadrons are comprised of combat controllers and pararescuemen. These men are proficient in sea-air-land insertion tactics into forward, nonpermissive environments. The CCTs establish assault zones with an air traffic control capability. Assault zones could be a drop zone for a parachute deployment, a landing zone for heliborne operations, or a follow on fixed-wing aircraft. It could also be an extraction or low-level resupply.

The CCTs specialize in air traffic control. When it is given the "go" signal, it can place numerous forms of lights—visible and infrared—that can be controlled by CCT members as easily as you would use your TV remote on your home theater system. The combat control teams are also responsible for ground-based fire control of the AC-130 Spectre gunships and helicopters of AFSOC, as well as for all air assets, including Army and Navy aircraft. In addition to these capabilities, CCTs provide vital command and control capabilities in the forward AO and area qualified in demolition to remove obstructions and obstacles to the landing or drop zone.

The ratio of CCTs to PJs will vary with the mission profile and who the STT will be attached with (i.e., Rangers, SEALs, Special Forces, and so on). If the mission is a combat search and rescue, then the team would be pararescue jumper "heavy"; whereas, if the task is to take down an airfield and hold it, the team would then be made up primarily of CCTs. Each mission profile is unique and the Special Tactics Teams are highly skilled in overcoming, adapting, and improvising to meet their objectives.

While the combat controllers are busy with their tasks, the PJs provide any emergency medical care necessary to stabilize and evacuate injured personnel. The PJs are the ones who will establish the overall combat search and rescue operations, planning, and procedures. The pararescue men of the STS will provide

Skilled in the art of small unit tactics, a CCT and PJ patrol the brush, performing a reconnaissance and surveillance. With weapons at the ready, they are poised to engage any threat crossing their path.

Having reached his recon position, this combat controller uses a PRC-117 SATCOM radio to communicate information back to headquarters. Across his knee rests his M-4 rifle.

Special Tactics Squadrons are a combination of combat controllers and pararescuemen. These highly trained teams are experts in ATC, CAS, and emergency trauma medicine. They can often be found attached with U.S. Army Special Forces, Rangers, and SEALs and have been known to operate with British SAS units.

triage and medical treatment for follow-on forces. To say that these individuals are highly skilled would be an understatement. They are instructed in the latest medical procedures in combat and trauma medicine. When they are not jumping into remote hostile environments, or in training in a joint task force field training exercise (FTX), you might find them riding along with EMS units in large urban areas. Such cities

have high incidents of gunshots wounds and similar injuries, so they may get further experience to take into the field.

During Operation Just Cause, the Special Tactics Squadrons were with the Rangers in the raid on Rio Hato. CCTs perform air traffic control and Special Air assets fire control. PJs were there to provide emergency medical assistance and triage evaluation with the Rangers. CCT members were also with SEAL Team 4 at Patilla Airport.

CCTs provided the air traffic control in Saudi Arabia and virtually ran the King Fihad Airport during Desert Shield and Storm. At the beginning of "The Storm" they were with the SF troops that opened the air corridor for U.S. and coalitions aircraft.

It was three sergeants of the 24th STS that were with the Rangers in Somalia. Here is a prime example of the exploitation of talents of the Special Tactics Squadron members. The CCTs would call in air fire within meters of their position. They would literally blow out one wall, then another, and thus were able to evade and escape (E&E) out of harm's way. For their actions during the firefight, TSgt. Tim Wilkinson was awarded the Air Force Cross for extraordinary heroism, MSgt. Jeffery Bray, received Silver Stars for gallantry.

During Operation Restore Democracy, while network news crews showed the U.S. helicopters settling into an LZ in Haiti and being heralded as "... the first Americans to land on Haitian soil," members of the AFSOC/STS had already been on the ground for days, surveying HLZ and setting up lighting for the heliborne troopers.

There are six STS units worldwide, with approximately 300 combat controllers and pararescue jumpers combined throughout the Air Force. The 21st STS is stationed at Fort Bragg, North Carolina; the 24th STS is at Pope Air Force Base, North Carolina; the 22nd STS is at McChord Air Force Base, Washington; the 23rd is at Hurlburt Field, Florida; the 320th STS is at Kadena Air Base, Japan; and the 321st STS is at RAF Mildenhall, England. Each squadron has three teams; each team comprises 18 enlisted and 2 officers. One half of the team will be qualified as combat controllers (CCT) and the other half pararescue (PJ). Currently there are more combat controllers in the squadron than there are PJs.

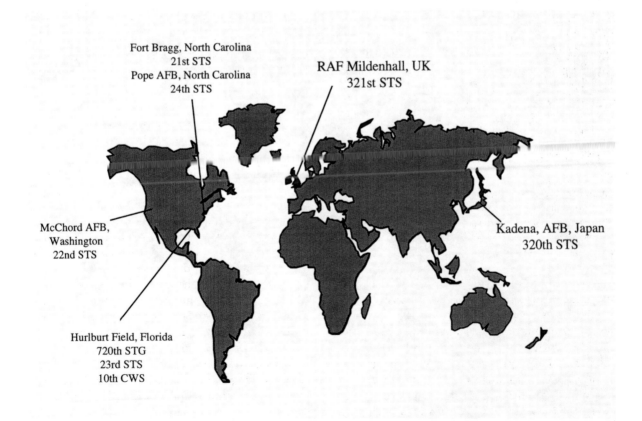

Fort Bragg, North Carolina
21st STS
Pope AFB, North Carolina
24th STS

RAF Mildenhall, UK
321st STS

McChord AFB,
Washington
22nd STS

Kadena, AFB, Japan
320th STS

Hurlburt Field, Florida
720th STG
23rd STS
10th CWS

The extreme in low-level insertion, going in on foot. STTs are trained to use GPS, maps, compasses, and even the stars to navigate from point-to-point to accomplish their mission. If you look under the floppy hats, you can see the "secrette," the communications headgear used with the interteam radios, in this case an AN/PRC-126. These two STS team members wear a new type of 3-D camouflage. This "cammo" has leaf patterns attached to break up any silhouette and allow them to disappear into the surrounding foliage.

Pararescue Origins

Today's pararescuemen can trace their lineage back to a remote jungle close to the China-Burma border during a summer in World War II. Here 21 persons were forced to bail out of a disabled C-46 in the hot August of 1943. The area was so isolated that the only possible way to get to the survivors was a parachute drop. Lieutenant Colonel Don Fleckinger, along with two medical personnel, volunteered to make the jump. From this mission the concept of pararescue was born.

In the early fifties, with the formation of the Air Rescue Service, and subsequently in 1956, into the reorganized Air Rescue and Recovery Service, PJs, or *para-jumpers* as the name denotes, have been prepared to make the ultimate sacrifice to uphold their motto, "That Others May Live." Trained in parachuting, mountaineering, and medical techniques, these men would provide the rescue capability for both military and civilian rescues.

U.S. Air Force PJs have also been instrumental in the recovery of astronauts in the space program of the United States. Pararescuemen have worked with NASA since the early Gemini programs of the sixties. They were present to support Skylab missions and currently are on call to provide rescue support to the space shuttle program.

It was in 1966 that Air Force Chief of Staff General John P. McConnell approved the wearing of the maroon beret for pararescue forces. The maroon beret symbolizes the blood sacrifices by PJs and their devotion to duty in coming to the aid of others.

A considerable benefit to the PJs was the introduction of combining parachuting capability with scuba techniques. It is not uncommon for a pararescueman to be loaded with up to 100 pounds of equipment when he is ready to make his jump. According to Master Sergeant Ron Childress (ret.), "It was not uncommon for the PJs to put the survivor on the penetrator under heavy fire and be killed in action . . . to effect the survivor recovery."

During the Vietnam War, PJs accompanied the Jolly Green helicopters in the search and rescue of downed pilots. These men operated the jungle penetrators as well as the onboard weapons. It was not uncommon for a PJ to ride the hoist down to an injured pilot, with M-16 in hand, and secure the wounded man to the penetrator and hold him secure as they rode back up to the relative safety of the hovering helicopter.

During Operation Just Cause in 1989, pararescuemen were among the first U.S. combatants to parachute into Panama. Their medical expertise was called upon continually during this short operation, as they recovered and treated the majority of U.S. Army Rangers who had taken two Panamanian airfields in the first hours of the invasion. Speeding up and down the runway in their specially designed Rescue All Terrain Transport (RATT), the PJs collected the casualties and brought them to a collection point.

At this location the pararesuemen performed triage and provided the necessary medical attention until MedEvac could be arranged. All this time firefights were going on around them while they cared for their wounded.

The PJs were on call during Operations Desert Shield and Desert Storm in the Persian Gulf. It was during the Gulf War that the pararescuemen would penetrate into hostile territory to recover a downed F-14 navigator. Pararescue also provided support for the airlift operations after the war to the Kurdish refugees fleeing into northern Iraq.

The training of a pararescueman is a constant process. They continuously endeavor to perfect current techniques as well as develop new procedures. Whether scaling the face of a mountain, doing a HALO jump at 25,000 feet, racing down the tarmac of some foreign airfield, or suspended from a cable of an MH-53 Pave Low over a distressed vessel in the Pacific, the PJs will accomplish their tasks at all costs.

CCT Origins

The need for combat controllers surfaced in the early air campaigns of World War II. During several major parachute assaults, the paratroopers fell short of their drop zone. This resulted in troopers being scattered as much as 30 miles from the drop zone. It became quite evident that effective guidance and control of the air transports were required. The Army created and trained a company-sized group of scouts that were parachute qualified. This unit became known as Pathfinders. Their mission was to precede the main assault force to the drop zone. Once on the ground they would use lights, flares, and smoke pots to provide a visual guide and weather information to the incoming planes.

In the fall of 1943 Pathfinders were first employed during the airborne reinforcement of allied troops in Italy. Minutes before the main body reached the designated area, the Pathfinders hit the ground and established the drop zone for the follow-on paratroops. These CCT forerunners, the Pathfinders, proved instrumental in the D-Day invasion of Europe as they prepared the way for elements of the 82nd and 101st Airborne Divisions.

On 18 September 1947 the U.S. Air Force was officially established. The Air Force assumed responsibility for tactical airlift support of U.S. Army forces. U.S. Air Force Pathfinders were later

The water is unforgiving. Those going into STS will learn the latest techniques in open-circuit SCUBA and closed-circuit systems such as the Draeger rebreather. Here a combat controller emerges from the water wearing a LAR-V rebreather. The LAR-V will leave no telltale bubbles on the water's surface to give away the STT location during an underwater insertion.

STARS

Ask the average person in the civilian community about special operations and you'll get answers that vary from Hollywood's image of Rambo to martial arts masters, from legendary Green Berets to the new folk heroes the U.S. Navy SEALs. Ask the representative members of the U.S. military, including some theater commanders, and they'll most likely expand that list to include Army Rangers. Few people, even in the military, are aware that the U.S. Air Force has one of the most elite ground units in the United States special operations arsenal, the Special Tactics Squadron.

Sergeant Bob Benton of 23rd STS related that there are commanders that , ". . . just don't know we exist. However, when they find out what we are capable of, then they constantly request us." The issue is, there are not enough STS teams to fill every commander's request.

It is not a matter of these Air Commandos wanting to be in the spotlight. On the contrary, they prefer their anonymity. Working in the shadows in a hostile environment makes survival favor them and gives their missions a higher percentage of success if no one knows they exist. Benton continues, "This is a two-edge sword. What this also means is that we have a hard time getting recruits for the program. Some of the [Air Force] recruiters don't even know we're out here."

Enter the U.S. Air Force STARS, special tactics and rescue specialists formed from the ranks of the 720th STS. They perform at air shows and other high-visibility functions to present the people with a view of AFSOC's capabilities. On one occasion they even parachuted a team into an NFL game.

The STARS are a demonstration team, goodwill ambassadors, and a recruiter's dream, much like the U.S. Air Force's demonstration squadron, the Thunderbirds. Unlike the Thunderbirds, however, the STARS also have full-time assignments within AFSOC. The 30 jumpers belong to operational squadrons at Pope Air Force Base, McChord Air Force Base, and Hurlburt Field. These highly trained Air Force PR teams could be jumping in an air show in Dayton, Ohio, today and then deploying into a real-world hot spot on the other side of the globe tomorrow. (You won't find the Thunderbirds doing a CAP the day after one of their demonstrations.) As expressed in their recruitment brochures, these STS troops are "Air Force with an Attitude."

Wayne Norrad is the STARS' coordinator and a retired CCT, chief master sergeant. If you saw the Harrison Ford movie, *Air Force One*, you would be familiar with Norrad's work. It was his idea for the rescue scene between the Combat Talon and the "president's" plane.

Next time you see a parachute team dropping onto the 50-yard line or the tarmac at an air show, look carefully. There's a good chance those skydivers are AFSOC STARS. Norrad reports that they're even looking into a STARS song. Perhaps it's time to add the scarlet and maroon berets of the U.S. Air Force Special Operations Command to America's folk heroes.

called combat control teams and were activated in January 1953. This newly organized group provided navigational aids and air traffic control for the expanding airlift forces. These teams remained under aerial port squadrons until 1977. In 1984 CCTs were restructured and assigned to the numbered Air Forces (i.e., 8th Air Force and so on), and in 1991 they were placed under the control of host wing commanders.

Since their activation, CCTs have seen action worldwide. Combat controllers participated in the Lebanon crisis (July–October 1958), the Congo

Land navigation is essential to the skills of an STS member. Both PJs and combat controllers will become experts in using a map and a compass. They will also become familiar with celestial navigation using the stars. While they are issued GPS units and are quite adept in their use, they must always be able to travel from point-to-point while relying on low-tech alternatives.

Special Tactics Squadron teams receive military free fall training at Fort Bragg and Yuma Proving Grounds. Wearing a Gentex helmet with oxygen in place, this PJ is suited up and "good to go"! He is armed with a Colt M-4 rifle and an ACOG scope mounted on top, in place of the carrying handle.

uprising (July–October 1960), the Cuban Missile Crisis (October 1962), the China-India confrontation (November 1962–September 1963), and during the Vietnam War (1967–1975).

It was also during the Vietnam War that the CCTs emerged as one of the Air Force's premiere units. Their exploits in Southeast Asia helped form the basis of current combat control operating methods.

They were qualified as air traffic controllers, parachutists, and in emergency first aid. They also received training in communications, small unit patrolling techniques, and ambush and counterambush tactics. It was the CCTs who established drop zones and landing zones. Here the basis of operating methods were developed and refined as used by today's combat control teams.

Combat control teams could be found collocated in isolated Army Special Forces camps scattered throughout Vietnam. Here these air commandos called in air strikes to support the Green Beret camps, or guide a C-123 Fairchild or C-130 Hercules down the airstrip for a much-needed resupply run. Such beginnings have evolved into the close bond between the STS units and other special operation forces.

It has been reported that combat control teams were used in clandestine missions near the Ho Chi Minh Trail. These special operations troops would locate enemy convoys, then call in Air Commando gunships, such as "Puff," "Spooky," or other Spectres, to attack the column, thus severing the communist

Airborne! All members of the Special Tactics Squadron are airborne-qualified. They will go through three weeks of training at the Basic Airborne School at Fort Benning, Georgia. Upon completion of five jumps, they will be awarded the coveted silver wings.

supply line to the south and the North Vietnamese Army (NVA).

From 1967 through 1972 combat controllers saw action throughout the Vietnam theater of operations. They assured mission safety, expedited air traffic flow, and coordinated with airlift control units. CCTs were the last troops to be evacuated from the beleaguered outpost at Khe Sahn. Two U.S. Air Force combat controllers were among the

last Americans to be airlifted from the U.S. Embassy when Saigon fell in 1975.

Prior to Operation Eagle Claw, a lone combat controller performed R&S of Desert Site One. The mission planners had scores of aerial photographs, but they needed HUMINT, someone on the ground. In early April 1980, Major John T. Carney Jr. was delivered to the Iranian wasteland via a Central Intelligence Agency aircraft.

The major pulled a small motorcycle from the plane. Equipped with a pair of night vision goggles, a shovel, and some beacons, he began to survey the proposed landing site. Maj. Carney paused from time to time to take a core sample of the desert sand. This was later analyzed to determine if the location could support the weight of the Sea Stallions and Hercules that would bring in Col. Beckwith's rescue force.

It was for this mission that the "Box and One" lighting method was developed. Setting up his strobes in a box pattern approximately 90 feet apart, then placing the fifth at the end of the landing zone 5,000 feet away, marked the end of the LZ. Thus Maj. Carney's team of combat controllers had given him a tool where five strobes would do the job that was normally done by more than two dozen. With the light bags burred below the surface, Carney took one more survey of the area before loading his motorcycle into the CIA Otter and extracting from Iran.

When the aircraft containing the assault force arrived for the actual mission, the pilots hit the remote and the five lights lit up the landing zone below. The mission of the combat controller was a success, one of the few of Operation Eagle Claw. Operation Rice Bowl, the planning of the rescue mission and the successful execution of the R&S by Major Carney, is viewed by those in the AFSOC as the birth of the Special Tactics Teams.

Combat controllers jumped with the Army Rangers in Grenada in Operation Urgent Fury in 1983 and again as the United States invaded Panama in 1989 in Operation Just Cause. While their PJ teammates tended the wounded, CCTs called in air strikes from AC-130H gunships in support of the Rangers' operations.

Whether it was on a trodden-down cow pasture in Europe in World War II where they lit smoke pots to mark the landing field, an isolated Special Forces camp in the central highlands of Vietnam, or the all-out war of Desert Storm, combat controllers have been and continue to be an integral part of the success of special operations.

Today, combat control teams are ground combat forces assigned to the Special Tactics Squadrons of the U.S. Air Force Special Operations Command. These highly trained CCTs are organized and equipped to establish and control the air-ground interface in the objective area rapidly. These functions include assault zone assessment and establishment, air traffic control command and control communications, and special operations terminal attack control. In the event that the runway or airfield must be cleared of obstacles, the CCT units are trained in removal and equipped with demolitions that allow them to accomplish such a task. Combat control teams may be deployed with air and ground forces in the execution of direct action, special reconnaissance, austere airfield, combat search and rescue, counterterrorism, foreign internal defense and humanitarian assistance operations.

Combat controllers' roles and responsibilities are to plan, organize, supervise, and establish air traffic control at forward airheads. They will select or assist in selecting sites and marking assault zones (drop, landing, or recovery) with visual and electronic navigational aids for day and night airland and airdrop operations. The CCT will operate portable and mobile communications equipment and terminal and en route air navigation aids required to control and support air traffic in these forward areas. These teams will evaluate and relay status of assault zones to inbound aircraft as well as higher headquarters. Such reports may include limited weather observations, including surface and altitude wind data, temperature, and cloud heights. CCTs control

This Pararescue sergeant administers an IV to a wounded team member. Pararescuemen are highly trained in dealing with the numerous types of injuries they may encounter. They are also trained in the latest methods of trauma medicine. They undergo the same training that U.S. Army Special Forces medics attend. From simple procedures to the treatment of gunshot wounds, the pararescuemen are tops in their fields.

vehicular traffic in the airport area, in the air and on the runway and taxiways. They also monitor air navigational aids and maintain qualification of primary assigned weapons.

The CCT on the ground is "the" air traffic controller. He regulates en route and airhead air traffic and initiates, coordinates, and issues air traffic control clearances, holding instructions, and advisories to maintain aircraft separation and promote safe, orderly, and expeditious air traffic flow under visual or nonradar flight rules. Whether using the radio in his truck or the Tactical Air Navigation (TACAN) unit attached to the rear of a quad, he conducts ground-to-air communication. Visual and electronic systems are used to control and expedite the movement of aircraft while en route, arriving, and departing from the airhead. The CCT will interface with pilots, issuing advisories on air traffic control, weather, and wake turbulence. He directs actions in handling aircraft emergencies during Special Tactics Team deployments to support contingency

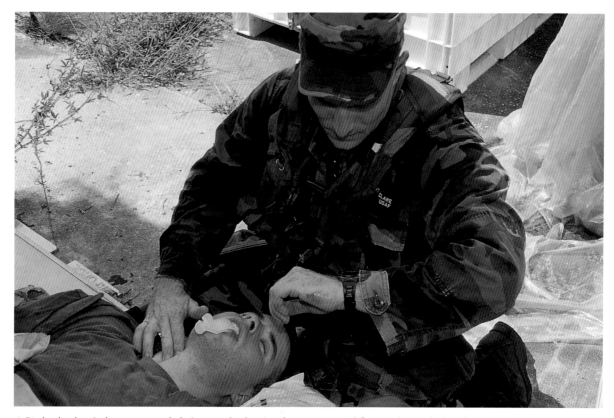

A PJ checks the vitals on a wounded airman who has just been evacuated from a downed aircraft. Pararescuemen must learn to evaluate, stabilize, and extract their wounded fast, often under enemy fire.

operations. He'll coordinate clearances, instructions, advisors, and air traffic movement with forward and rear area commanders. Combat controllers are instrumental in providing close air support with AFSOC assets. Combat controllers may receive advance training and become qualified in special operations tactical air control (SOTAC), allowing them to provide CAS with the "fast movers."

Further, the CCT establishes and operates forward communication facilities and supervises and establishes high-frequency, satellite, or other long-range C4I links between forward and rear area commanders. The CCT will develop terminal instrument procedures for assault zones, including gathering current ground intelligence in forward airhead areas. Combat controllers coordinate with pararescue personnel on casualty and patient staging and collection point for expeditious MedEvac.

Special tactics squadron combat controllers may be deployed into forward area and forward operating locations in special operation missions, CSAR, and fire support duties. Along with the removal of obstacles with explosives, there may be an occasion when the CCT would be called upon to "sanitize" a crash site. While the task of "blowing up" a downed aircraft normally falls under the responsibility of other operators (i.e., Rangers, SEALs, Special Forces, and so on), CCTs are fully capable of carrying out such a task if necessary. The special tactics CCTs are definitely one of the USSOCOM's most lethal weapons.

Selection—PAST and Phase Tests

The first step in the long process in becoming a member of the elite Special Tactics Squadron begins with selection. A physical abilities and stamina test, or PAST, is the beginning for all Air Force personnel for access to combat control and pararescue training. This is the starting point for both officers and enlisted people; regular Air Force as well as Air National Guard (ANG) and Reserve. The test is administered and must be completed in a three-hour time frame. If candidates are unable to meet any of the minimum standards, they fail and the testing is terminated at that point.

PAST has a predetermined Standard Operating Procedure (SOP) and is not to be altered. This test begins with a 25-meter underwater swim. The applicant is given a demonstration of the task, then enters the water wearing only a swimsuit and goggles. If at any time the applicant breaks the water's surface he has failed and the test is over.

Accomplishing the underwater swim, the candidate is given a short rest (5 to 10 minutes), then is back in the water. This time it's for a 1,000-meter surface swim. With no additional equipment than the underwater test, the candidate begins this part of the test. Using either a free-style or side stroke, he will have up to 26 minutes to complete the swim. The surface swim must be continuous. If the candidate stops at anytime during the test, the test is over and considered a failure for the entire PAST. After the completion of the surface swim, the candidate is given the luxury of a 30-minute rest before continuing.

Exchanging a swimming suit for a running outfit and a reliable pair of running shoes, the candidate will embark on a 1.5-mile run. The maximum time for the run is 10 minutes and 30 seconds. The run is graded like the surface swim. It must be continuous,

This pararescueman uses the REDS, or rapid extrication device system, on a downed helicopter to aid in the extraction of the pilot from the aircraft. Similar to the jaws of life carried by various fire departments, this equipment can cut and chew its way through metal, wires, and airframe to get to a crewmember.

no stopping. If the trooper stops anytime during the run, the test is over and considered a failure of the entire PAST. On completion of the run, there is a 10-minute cooling off time, then on to calisthenics.

Four calisthenics will be exercised and evaluated, each with an allotted time and exercise form required. Exercise form is strictly enforced, so if the candidate makes it to the pipeline, it is extremely important to

Upon graduation from the pararescue school, the PJ is awarded the maroon beret with the pararescue crest, "That Others May Live."

get this right here first. A three-minute break is given between each exercise.

Chinups, 8 in 1 minute, are next. If the applicant falls off, stops, or releases the bar prior to completion, the exercise is terminated. Next, it's sit-ups, 50 in 2 minutes. There is no rest position for this exercise; to rest is to fail. Next, it's push-ups, 50 in 2 minutes. If the knees touch the ground, if the buttocks raises into the air, if the stomach sags to the ground or a hand or foot is raised from starting position, the test is terminated. Finally, it's flutter kicks, 50 in 2 minutes. Starting with feet and head roughly 6 inches off the ground, hands under buttocks to support the lower back, the candidate begins: raising the left leg, then the right to approximately a 45-degree angle, while returning the left to starting position, then repeat. The exercise will continue until muscle failure or time completion. This final exercise is vital to the underwater warrior. It will be used in subsequent training and actual missions; the STS trooper will use the flutter kicks to count off and pace distances underwater. These techniques must be mastered, for the sea is a most unforgiving environment of special operation missions.

Having successfully completed the PAST, our candidate has proven they are *capable* of enduring the quelling training they will be subject to upon entering the Indoctrination Course at Lackland Air Force Base, San Antonio, Texas. For enlisted personnel, they are ready to move on to the Indoctrination Course.

Phases I and II
Officers seeking to continue to indoctrination and the pipeline still have some work to do before they can embark to Lackland. Officers must write a narrative on "Why I Want to Be a Combat Controller." They must also obtain three letters of recommendation. These letters must comment on leadership abilities and come from their chain-of-command, a recent commander, or other pertinent individuals. Along with these recommendations, they must submit Officer Performance reports, Enlisted Performance reports, and Training Profiles, verification of successful completion of PAST, medical records, and tests all too numerous to mention. At this point the officer must also volunteer for hazardous duty.

With this all done, they may submit their request. This is referred to as Phase I. Here a board of four field-grade officers will meet and evaluate the volunteers. They will determine out of the requesting officers the top 15 to 20 percent who will be selected to attend Phase II.

Phase II is an additional selection process conducted at Pope Air Force Base, North Carolina. Candidates will complete various activities and will be evaluated on their performance. Here the 324th Training Squadron will put them through classes in underwater swimming, which will also provide a prelude to competency in scuba.

Special tactics squadron teams must be at home in the water. Phase II is set up to accomplish this level of comfort by subjecting the candidates to the water confidence training. From simple but valuable lessons in clearing a flooded mask to the SEAL specialty of drownproofing, the potential

STS officers will spend a great deal of their time in, on, and under the water. During such training as buddy breathing, the instructors will introduce "stress" factors in the form of pool harassment. For example, while practicing buddy breathing the instructor may try to take away their snorkel, or remove their masks, force students underwater, or other techniques as they see fit. All the time the officer is being evaluated on their reactions: Is he calm, can he maintain control?

Drownproofing is not for the faint of heart and is an essential asset to an SOF warrior, whether Navy SEAL or AFSOC STS. In drownproofing, the students' wrists and ankles are secured together with ropes or Velcro straps. Once bound, they enter the water and begin the task of drownproofing. This is accomplished by bobbing, floating, traveling, flips, and recovery. Each segment of the training is under the careful eye of the instructor, as well as a safety swimmer in SCUBA gear, just in case. Next comes treading water, using their legs to maintain positive bouancy on the water's surface, without using their arms and hands.

Phase II is rounded out with a minimum 6-mile march carrying a 40- to 60-pound rucksack, multiple calisthenics sessions, leadership reaction courses, psychological evacuations, and briefing and writing techniques. Those officers who successfully complete Phase II and are selected by the board are "good to go" and may now head to Lackland.

INDOCTRINATION

Ask U.S. Navy SEALs what bonds them together, whether enlisted or officer, young or old, and they will tell you it is BUDS—Basic Underwater Demolition/SEAL training. Talk with a member of a U.S. Army Special Forces Operational A Detachment (A-Team) and they'll tell you it's the Q-Course, the qualification course. For the members of the Special Tactics Squadrons it is the Indoctrination Course.

The journey into the Special Tactics Squadrons begins in the hot Texas sun, near San Antonio, at Lackland Air Force Base. For 12 grueling weeks

With strobe, radio, and weapon, this CCT is ready to execute his mission regardless of the difficulties. His training has taught him to drive on no matter what circumstances come his way.

potential team members go through the Pararescue/Combat Control Indoctrination Course, or as Operations Location-Hotel, as it is referred to by the STTs. Here the volunteers show whether they have what it takes to enter into the highly selective, extremely aggressive, and high-risk world of Air Force special operations.

The Indoctrination Course, or OL-H, selects, screens, and trains the potential PJs and CCTs for their specialty fields. The candidate is at the threshold of a 55-week journey through some of the military's most intensive training. Indoctrination is designed to push the students mentally and physically to their limits and beyond. This training prepares them for the high standards they will be expected to meet as they make their way through the pipeline and their ultimate assignment—combat. During IC the instructors will place the students in highly stressful situations that will challenge their mental capabilities, their physical qualities, and most important, their determination and perseverance to stick it out until the job is done. There is no room in STS or any other SOF unit for an individual who wants to quit when

The standard-issue Strobe and IR cover carried by STS operators. While common among all U.S. Special Operations Forces, you will often find STS CCT carrying a number of these to facilitate ATC and other ground-to-air signaling.

things get rough. Students who graduate from the Indoctrination Course will have developed the skills that should prevent them from failure in the pipeline if they give and maintain 100 percent dedication.

For the next 12 weeks the candidates will hone themselves to a mental and physical razor's edge. Run training consists of long, slow distances, sprints, interval training, and others. The pace for evaluation is a seven-minute mile. Weight training programs are included to develop strength, endurance, and speed. Interspersed between these activities comes calisthenics, assorted, at the judgment of the instructors.

In week three the trainees experience "Motivation Week" or "Hell Week." Actually three days, it seems like a week, one that is never going to end. One moment our trainees are resting in their bunks and the next moment they are belly down, face in the dirt, crawling under barbed wire through the obstacle course. The exercise goes on nonstop: no sleep, pushing the envelope of their inner strength. Motivation Week separates the overwhelmed from the serious operators. Hell Week cuts the class size; it is not unheard of that out of a class of 80, 9 volunteers graduate. That's an

attrition rate of 90 percent! There was one class that graduated only 2 individuals.

From day one and throughout IC, the candidates will find themselves in the water. Here the candidates are subjected to water confidence and swim training. This is the same training that the officer students were exposed to in Phase II. At indoctrination, the enlisted get their feet wet, literally, as they learn underwater swimming; fin swimming; mask and snorkel recovery; buddy breathing/pool harassment; bobbing; underwater knots; ditch and donning equipment; treading water; weight belt swim; and the ever-popular drownproofing. For the officer trainees, they get to appreciate this course a second time; practice does make perfect!

The course also will concentrate on marksmanship training (M-16A1 rifle and M-9 pistol), physiological training (altitude and dive chambers), as well as academic instruction in dive physics and metric measurements. Upon graduation from this selection process, the airmen and officers now have their ticket to ride the pipeline, and they will move on to numerous military specialty schools.

The Pipeline

The pipeline lasts 12 to 15 months, depending on the specialty. It is designed to transform an airman or officer into a highly motivated weapons system.

First stop in the pipeline after IC or OL-H is the U.S. Army Combat Divers School in Key West, Florida. At this location, our candidate learn to use SCUBA gear to stealthily infiltrate a target area. This training is essential to the STS teams since they are often tasked with supporting U.S. Navy SEALs and must be at home in the water, as are the frogmen.

Training will include waterborne operations both day and night. Students will be taught ocean subsurface navigation, deep diving techniques, marine hazards, and how to read tides, waves, and currents. It will be in Key West that they'll be instructed in the proper procedures of submarine lock-in and lock-out, the method of entering and exiting a submerged sub. Training in both open-circuit and closed-circuit equipment will be taught. This is not recreation diving as depths in training go down to 120 feet under diverse operating conditions.

This training phase will last four weeks. Week one begins with physical training and further physical conditioning to get the trainee prepared for the balance of the class. Week two will find the PJ/CCT in familiar territory, an extension of the instruction given in the water confidence and swim training at Lackland. In week three, they will dive, dive, and then dive some more.

In the final week trainees will perform an underwater compass swim. It is not sufficient to just know "how" to SCUBA dive, they must be able to execute a mission via underwater egress. Equipped with a compass board, SCUBA tank, weapon, and rucksack they will carry out an infiltration to a point on the beach. The final week also brings more night dives, a field training exercise, and graduation.

While still in the neighborhood, our warrior will attend the U.S. Navy Underwater Egress Training at Pensacola NAS, Florida. Here the future STT members learn the proper techniques to safely escape from a sinking or submerged aircraft. The Navy instructors will teach principles, procedures, and proper techniques to accomplish this task. This training helps to instill confidence in the men and make them as comfortable in the water as possible.

Future pararescuemen and combat controllers will partake in multiple exercises using the HEEDS, or Helicopter Emergency Egress Device System. The cadre simply call it the "dunking machine" or "dunker," because that's what it does. It is a drumlike simulator that can be fitted to several configurations: two-seat, four-seat, or passenger compartment. The students get in and fasten their seat belts. The "dunker" is raised to approximately 8 feet above the water's surface and dropped. This simulates the ditching of a helicopter, and the student experiences what it feels like to be in a sinking aircraft. During this training one scenario will have the

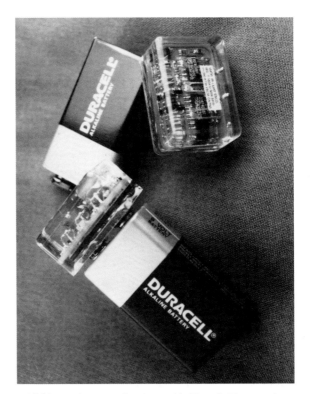

Weighing only a mere 2 ounces, this Phoenix IR transmitter is used by STS teams in covert operations. Invisible to the naked eye, with NVGs it can be seen up to 20 miles away. It is powered by a 9-volt battery, lightweight and easy to use. The Phoenix Jr. is a simple on/off strobe. The advanced unit contains two protruding pins allowing the unit to be programmed with a varying series of patterns.

HEEDS sink and roll over; now the PJs are underwater and upside down. Another exercise will have them submerged while they are wearing black-out goggles. Such a situation could cause most people to panic, but future pararescuemen must remain calm and proficient even in a sinking helo; it is their job to save lives and lead the survivors to safety.

Next stop in the pipeline after IC is Fort Benning, Georgia, U.S. Army Airborne School. Here for the next three weeks trainees will be at the mercy

Basic airborne training is broken into three weeks: Ground, Tower, and Jump Week. During Ground Week our trainees will start an intensive program of instruction designed to prepare the troopers to complete their parachute jumps. They will learn how to execute a flawless parachute landing fall (PLF) to land safely in the LZ. The PLF consists of five points of contact designed to absorb the shock of landing and distribute it across the (1) balls of the feet, (2) calf, (3) thigh, (4) buttocks, and (5) the push-up muscle of the back. They will learn the proper way to exit an aircraft using mock-ups of a C-130 and a C-141. They will climb up a 34-foot tower; here they will be connected to the lateral drift apparatus (LDA) and upon command will assume door position and "Jump!" Proper body position will be evaluated, and they'll do it over and over until the "Black Hats" are happy; and they will run.

Next comes Tower Week. Now that our trainees have learned how to exit, position, and land, they will have this week to refine those skills. Using a training device known as the swing landing tower (SLT) where they are hooked up to a parachute harness, they jump from a 12-foot-high elevated platform. The apparatus provides the downward motion and oscillation simulating that of an actual parachute jump. To make things more challenging for the student, the instructors have control of the SLT and can determine if they want to land hard or soft. As one student rushes toward the ground, hands clinging to the harness, the instructor yells, "Hazard left!" and leans into the rope controlling the drop. They watch as the airborne trainee hits the ground, and they better have landed in a manner to avoid the imaginary obstacle, or the "Airborne Sergeant" will have a few choice words and a number of push-ups, too. "Airborne!"

During week two the student gets to ride the "Tower." The Tower is designed to give the student practice in controlling the parachute during the decent from 250 feet and execute a PLF upon landing. They will learn how to handle parachute malfunctions, and they will run.

If all else fails, there is always the old tried-and-true standby, the smoke grenade. While in the high-tech world of GPS and IR strobes, it is not uncommon to find a smoke grenade pack in the STT rucksack for signaling positions or marking an HLZ for pickup.

of the Army's "Black Hats," the Airborne instructors of the 1st Battalion (Airborne), 507th Parachute Infantry Regiment who will convert a "leg" into an "Airborne" trooper. They will learn what it takes to hurl oneself out of a perfectly good airplane for the purpose of infiltrating into a mission drop zone. They will become, "Motivated! Motivated!! Motivated!!!" and they will run, and when they cannot move another inch, they will run some more.

Finally, week three, Jump Week. The potential STS trooper will perform five parachute jumps. First, an individual jump with a T-10B. Next, a mass exit with equipment and T-10B chute. Then another individual exit with MC1-1B parachute and tactical assembly. The fourth jump will be a mass exit at night with T-10B and tactical equipment, and finally the fifth jump either an individual jump with an MV1-1B or mass jump with a T-10B parachute.

The U.S. Army's "Guide for Airborne Students" states, "Airborne training is a rite of passage for the warrior." Upon graduation they will be awarded the coveted Silver Wings and are now qualified as "Airborne" troopers.

Now that they have earned their "wings," it is off to Fort Bragg's U.S. Army Military Freefall Parachutist School. The mission of the school is to train personnel in the science of HALO, military free fall parachuting, and using the Ram-Air Parachute System (RAPS). Military free fall (MFF) parachuting enables the theater commander to infiltrate an STS team into an area that would prohibit the use of static-line parachute operations. Special operations missions require rapid and covert infiltration into operational areas.

During week one the future STS members will go through the normal in-processing and be issued equipment. At this time they will be assigned to a HALO instructor who will remain with them throughout the four-week training cycle. It is also during week one that they will be matched up with a "jump buddy." Their buddy will be approximately the same weight and height so they will fall at the same rate.

In ground school they will learn about the ram-air parachutes, substantially different from the usual T-10B or MCI-1B that they jumped with at Basic Airborne School. The MC-5, ram-air parachutes are rectangular as opposed to circular. These parachutes are extremely more maneuverable. Repacking procedures as well as rigging the parachutes and equipment will be taught in this phase of training. At this time, special jump com-

Combat controllers use an assortment of navigational aids for air traffic control. The VS-17 signal panel, measuring 72 by 19 inches, is colored international orange on one side and fluorescent pink on the other. Runway lights, red, green, blue, clear, and infrared can be controlled all from a small hand-held device.

mands will be covered as well as the use of the oxygen systems used for high-altitude jumping.

Emergency procedures (EPs) such as parachute malfunctions, cut-aways, entanglements, and so on are taught, and so is how to recover from these mishaps. These exercises are run through over and over until they become second nature to the jumpers. Falling at a rate of more than 180 feet per second, you do not have the luxury of thinking about the problem, you must react.

While in week one, the candidate will spend time in the Military Free Fall Simulator Facility. Completed in 1992 at Fort Bragg, at a cost of $5 million, this 11,000-square-foot facility contains an enclosed, vertical wind tunnel, 32-student classroom, operator control room, communications, and equipment rooms. "This facility is a marked improvement," relates Carol Darby of the Special Warfare School. "Prior to having the facility, the students had to practice [body stabilization] by laying on table tops."

The simulator is approximately 18 feet high and 14 feet in diameter and can support two jumpers with equipment up to 375 pounds. The simulator's fan

This combat controller prepares to set up the SATCOM antennae for the PRC-117 radio. While he is getting the unit ready, other members of the team have formed a defensive perimeter and are providing security for the team.

generates winds up to 132 miles per hour. Suspended in a column of air, the students will learn and practice body-stabilization techniques. The wind tunnel will simulate the effects of free falling at a speed of approximately 200 feet per second.

With ground week completed the students will travel to Yuma Proving Grounds, Arizona. Weeks two through five will find our candidates jumping, jumping, and jumping again, beginning at 10,000 feet with no equipment and working up to 25,000 feet with full equipment load and oxygen system. The course provides in-the-air instruction where the student will concentrate on stability, aerial maneuvers, and parachute deployment procedures. Each student will receive a minimum of 16 free-fall jumps; this will include 2 day and 2 night jumps with oxygen and full field equipment.

Now that our candidate has basked in the southern sun, the student will be whisked away to the northern climes of Washington state. For the next two and a half weeks at Fairchild Air Force Base, the student will attend the U.S. Air Force Survival School, home of the 336th Training Group. The mission of the school is *"To prepare America's aircrew for global survivability anytime, anywhere, and return with honor."* It was to this training that U.S. Air Force Captain Scott O'Grady credited his ability to survive on the ground after his F-16 was shot down in Bosnia.

Here in the mountains of Coville and Kanisksu national forests, approximately 70 miles north of Spokane, the cadre of the 22nd Training Squadron conducts the Combat Survival Training, basic survival techniques for remote areas. The course includes training in parachute landing falls (PLF), life support equipment procedures, construction of a shelter, procurement of food, and its preparation. Additional survival skills will be taught, such as day and night land navigation, ground-to-air signaling, vectoring rescue aircraft to their location, and helicopter hoist training—procedures, principles, equipment, and techniques that will be needed to survive the harshness of climate and hostile environment, with minimal equipment.

Along with the survival methods, they are also given SERE (Survival Escape Resistance and Evasion) training. These are methods in evasive travel, camouflage techniques, and resistance in captivity. During the SERE phase of training, students will participate in a field exercise where they will become familiar with captivity and interrogation. This training will challenge the future STS members physically, mentally, and emotionally. At the conclusion of the three weeks, they will have their debriefing and graduation.

Up to this point all airmen and officers go through the same training. Depending on training slots, the order of schools may vary. This training is the core skills of an STS team member. Now comes the time when they part ways and continue with either the pararescue course or the combat control path.

Pararescue Path

Those airmen continuing on the PJ program will attend the Special Operations Combat Medic Course at Fort Bragg. For the next 24 weeks they will undergo a program of concentrated medical training specifically designed for special operations medical personnel. This instruction will teach the prospective pararescuemen how to manage trauma patients prior to evacuation and provide medical treatment.

Students will actually be assigned to hands-on patient care both in emergency and hospital settings as part of their training. This is conducted during a four-week assignment in one of the country's largest metropolitan areas, New York City.

The course is divided into two stages: Phase I lasts five weeks and covers the Emergency Medical Technician Basic (EMT-B), and Phase II lasts 17 weeks. During this final phase, instruction is given in minor field surgery, pharmacology, combat trauma management, advance airway treatment, and military evacuation procedures.

To graduate, the student must become certified by the American Heart Association in Basic Life Support and Advanced Cardiac Life Support, as well as in Emergency Medical Technician-Basic and Paramedic levels with the National Registry of Emergency Medical Technicians in the United States.

Pararescue School

Having received their EMT-P certification, these future STS members will return to Kirtland Air Force Base, New Mexico. For the next 90 days they will undergo some of the most rigorous training available in the U.S. military. The Pararescue Recovery Specialist Course, the final course, which is uniquely tailored for pararescuemen, is divided into three phases: ground, air, and medical.

The future PJ receives quite extensive training and with good reason. A U.S. Army medic in the

Combat controller Staff Sergeant Rick Driggers of the 720th STS maintains radio communications with an orbiting MH-53E in preparation of a close air support mission. The other member of the STT carries an AN/PRC 117 multimission FM/AM UHF TACSAT radio.

Rangers, for example, is schooled in advanced combat medicine. He is fully capable of providing first aid treatment to his company during a mission. The medical specialists on a U.S. Army Special Forces A-Team are also highly trained. According to Carol Darby of the USASOC PAO, "Some SF medical sergeants who obtain the MOS of 18D can be as qualified as many physician assistants, maybe more." Although capable of providing combat medicine, their missions more often revolve around organizing medical care in civic actions, humanitarian operations, preventative medicine, and care of the A-Team members and indigenous guerrilla forces in unconventional warfare operations.

For pararescuemen assigned to AFSOC, though capable, their mission is not to perform fundamental first aid or civic actions. Special Tactics Squadron PJs do not have the comfort of working out of an aid station or having a Black Hawk sitting 10 yards away leisurely waiting for them. They have to get to the casualty, evaluate, stabilize, and extract, most likely while under hostile fire. Air Force Special Operations

The combat controllers are awarded the scarlet beret and the Air Force combat control crest, "First There."

PJs are proficient medical specialists who are fully trained as dive medics and excel in the science of trauma medicine.

The Air Force major commands have determined what qualifications pararescuemen must possess for assignment to their commands. Air Combat Command looks for an emergency medical technician–intermediant, while Air Force Special Operations Command requires its personnel to obtain the emergency medical technician–paramedic qualification. Medical training at Kirtland is specially designed to meet the U.S. Air Force requirements. Drive-along programs are included in the training regime. The PJs will accompany emergency rescue ambulance crews in various major cities. They will see the lacerations and punctures created by knife wounds, the blast and cavitations from gun shots, and fractures and crushing wounds found in vehicular accidents; in other words, trauma medicine.

Ground Phase

The student will be taught fieldcraft, firecraft, woodcraft, and accelerated survival techniques. Although the probability is rare, a PJ may be placed in a survival situation, on his own or with a wounded individual, perhaps a downed pilot. Trainees will learn how to live "off the land." Instruction will be given in identifying edible plants and how to obtain and prepare food from various wilderness sources. Master Sergeant Rick Weaver, an instructor at the Pararescue School, explains, "They [the students] have learned how to survive during the Air Force survival course. Now we want to see what they've learned. How do you start a fire? Show me how you get water from a pine branch by placing a plastic bag over it and squeezing off the moisture."

There may be times, for whatever reasons, that a PJ may be stuck on the ground alone. For this reason PJs are taught field operations and tactics at Kirtland. They are instructed in how to evade capture in enemy territory and how to survive. This exercise is a point-to-point movement; the student must locate and extract a casualty. While doing so, the school's cadre will be out looking for those in the field. The difference between this and the survival school is the evasion and escape exercises are not as intense at Kirtland. The cadre does not hunt you down and take you prisoner. It is designed to instill a confident outlook and positive attitude, to accept the circumstances, and "drive-on" at all cost.

Part of the ground phase includes lessons in navigation. Each candidate is required to be proficient in daylight or nighttime navigation. He must know the basics of geographics, how to read a map and navigate from one, and how to use a compass, a pace counter, and altimeter to determine his exact location. "The primary method of navigation," outlined by MSgt. Rick Weaver, "are the stars, lensatic compass, any compass, and a map. They must learn the basics." The Global Positioning System is taught, but it is used as a secondary method. However, as Weaver depicts, " . . . If you use it [GPS] all the time it will become a crutch." There are times when batteries go dead or the unit is not available. The student is expected to accomplish these skills in the darkest night with and without the aid of night vision goggles (NVGs). The trainee will be evaluated on his navigational prowess during a 10-day navigational exercise in a mountainous environment; well suited for such an exercise is the Manzano Mountains just south of Albuquerque, New Mexico.

While on the subject of mountains, the students will learn how to traverse, climb over, and rappel down a mountain. This may be done alone or with a casualty. During this phase of training they will become familiar with various mountaineering equipment, such as carabiners, chokes, ice axes, and so on. They will learn to tie more knots than a Boy Scout and how to work with ropes to build rope bridges. From belaying techniques to mountain walking, the trainees will become one with the mountain. Since mountains, as the sea, are unforgiving, it is this training that will result in a successful rescue, or the loss of a survivor and perhaps the rescue team.

The mountaineering instruction begins with "The Tower," a climbing and abseilling, or rappelling, structure 40-feet high. Here the students are given ample time to practice their climbing skills. The tower is arrayed with various "rocks" that lead to the top of it. This simulates climbing the mountain. The student must accomplish this task without the aid of sophisticated commercial mountaineering equipment. Once the climbing skills are accomplished, the instructors break out the latest "high-speed" climbing equipment for the trainees to learn. One might ask, why not bring out all this high-tech climbing gear right from the start? It is like learning long division; first you must know the basics, then you learn the short cuts. Pararescuemen have to accomplish their mission. Sometimes that includes using the latest mountaineering gear; other times, it means using their hands, arms, legs, and brains to complete the rescue.

As the trainees learn that what goes up must come down, they will learn the proper techniques in rappelling. How to rappel down the side of a mountain with a 90-pound rucksack or how to abseil down the side of a cliff with a wounded pilot in a stokes litter. He will also learn how to belay another climber down the face of the mountain.

Armed with the M-4 and M203 grenade launcher, this STT team leader provides cover as his team settles in for a regional survey. Note he is wearing three strobes: one pouch attached to his ALICE pack strap, one secured to his LBE, and a third sewn to the sleeve of his BDU. No matter how much equipment he may have to dump, he will still be able to execute his mission, and if needed evade and escape out of enemy territory.

Upon completion of the classroom work and the practicing on the tower, the candidates head out to the Pecos Mountains. Here for the next 10 days they will carry-out field and mountain operations. Upon arrival to the base of the mountain, they will establish a base camp from where operations will be carried out. There, instructors will give them further training in fieldcraft and land search.

Technical Sergeant Bart Decker, IFAM combat controller, establishes communication with the rest of his team as they await an in-bound Pave Low at Alpha 77, Eglin Air Force Base. The MH-53J will soon be overhead for a CAS mission. Although wearing a heavy ruck, Sgt. Decker makes maneuvering around the rooftop look like a walk in the park. STS troops know how to dig deep inside their gut and drive on regardless of the circumstances. The members of the AFSOC STS have a word describing that drive: U R R A H !

For the next four mornings they will head to the mountain for actual practice on the rocks. They rehearse basic rock climbing, ascending, rappelling, litter evacuations, river crossing, and improvised mountaineering setups. On the final day the instructors will evaluate all the trainees on every aspect of mountaineering. The student must pass all of these evaluations before he is allowed to continue the field training exercise.

The next five days of the operation will find the trainees practicing navigation and adverse terrain movement techniques as they traverse the mountain in planned routes. They will move from location to location and must become proficient in establishing their coordinates on a map. Students are required to ascertain their position within 50 meters at any time. This is to be done without the aid of a GPS unit. As the future PJs move along they will have more opportunities to practice fieldcraft skills. They will set up a camp, build a fire, forage for food, and be tasked with exercises ranging from building a rope bridge to treating a simulated casualty—all under the watchful eyes of their instructors. At the end of these five days they will be evaluated; those who pass move on to the next phase of training—Tactics.

STS teams, like other special operation forces, often operate in small groups, so they must learn small unit tactics. During the pararescue course this subject will be infused into the skills of the PJ. They will learn how to operate as a small team under extreme conditions. In addition, they will learn how to interface with other operators, such as SEALs, Rangers, Special Forces, and Special Air Service forces for quick integration.

While in this phase of training the students will be run through various scenarios and exercises planned by their instructors with an emphasis on night operations. A test of the small team unit integrity will come when the students face their instructors operating as an "OpForce." Will the team hold together, or will they break and run? You cannot have a quitter in a Special Tactics Squadron.

Ninety percent of the training mission will be performed at night. Some will use night vision goggles or devices extensively, while others will not. The trainees must learn how to operate with and without the aid of high-tech gear. This will teach them the benefits as well as the limitations of each scenario. Students are also instructed in the tactics of a nuclear, biological, and chemical (NBC) battle-field environment.

At the end of the Tactics phase of training, the candidates are sent on a three- to five-day tactical mission. This mission will test their skills in reaching their objective, perhaps a survivor, treating the casualty, preparing them to be moved, and evacuation.

All trainees will become familiar with various types of signaling and communications. They will learn how to improvise signals such as creating a signal out of wood or cloth panels. They will also receive training with the more sophisticated survival and long-range radios. Communications is one of the most essential tools in the PJs' selection of mission equipment.

Medical Phase

Individuals in the PJ career path are issued the standard ALICE (All-purpose Light Individual Carrying Equipment) field pack, size large. This is the same ruck found among SF A-Teams, Rangers, and fellow CCTs; the difference is that the PJ's ruck is replete with medical supplies. It's filled to the brim with a first aid kit, space blanket, surgical kit, tracheotomy kit, bandaging, IV infusor kit, diagnostic kit, poleless litter, assorted splints, stethoscope, medications, and so on. Each PJ's medical rucksack is arranged exactly the same, in the event a PJ would have to work out of another team member's pack. For example, the lower three large pockets on the outside of the rucksack are designated A, B, and C for *airway, bleeding,* and *circulation.* If any member of the team requires a battle dressing, he would know to go directly to the B, or lower, middle pocket. The PJ will be able to locate the needed items, when seconds may mean the difference between life and death. Other specialized medical equipment may be issued or transported with the STS team, dictated by mission parameters.

Team members will learn how to set up and properly wear their LBE (load-bearing equipment) and ALICE packs. It will not be uncommon for the medical rucks to weigh 90 or more pounds and the LBE to carry more than 20 pounds of gear. They will learn how to pack this gear and carry it as comfortably as possible. The PJs must learn how to move efficiently and stealthily under their load. They will have to learn how to navigate through an aircraft fuselage as well as through a wooded terrain or mountain slope.

Students will learn techniques and procedures on the use of the REDS, or Rapid Extraction Deployment System. Similar to the "jaws of life" found on fire trucks around the country, the REDS is used to cut away an aircraft fuselage to extricate a casualty. The REDS kit will contain a generator, combo tool, axes, reciprocal saw, and other necessary hardware to aid in the removal of the injured personnel. Students will also learn how to rig the REDS for fast rope.

While at Kirtland, the class will be taught how to conduct an actual search, from beginning the mission planning and implementation to the com-

On the ramp and ready to go, a RAMZ (rigged alternate method Zodiac) package is prepared to be deployed from an MC-130P Combat Shadow. Within seconds of the deflated Zodiac raft exiting the aircraft, the STT will follow it out. Once the team hits the water and has discarded its parachutes, team members begin removing the Zodiac from the packing, inflating the raft, and getting the outboard engine positioned, primed, and running. Once it is ready to go, they will load aboard and head for the insertion point.

With the four turboprop engines running, it is rather noisy inside a Combat Shadow. Communication is thereby conveyed in the form of hand signals. Here the jumpmaster for the RAMZ drop, Staff Sergeant Rick Driggers, holds up six fingers, indicating that the team is six minutes away from the insertion point. The cargo ramp will be opened and six minutes from now the STT will be in the air.

plete rescue and exfiltration. Using the information from their class, they will form into a rescue team, determine how to set up a base camp, and execute the mission of locating, treating, and evacuating a survivor.

Air Phase

The final phase of the Pararescue and Recovery Course is Air Operations. Here the trainees will become familiar with aircraft and aircrew knowledge: how to perform an aerial search pattern, emergency procedures, and various aircraft systems operations. The trainees will be taught AIE, alternate insertion/extraction methods. Helicopter techniques such as rope ladders, hoists, rappelling, and fast roping (from 30 to 120 feet) are all taught in this segment of training. The students will also learn how to helocast from helicopters. This entails deploying into the water from an altitude of approximately 10 feet at a rough speed of 10 knots.

Advanced parachuting techniques are taught in this phase. Students will learn how to rig their equipment with SCUBA tanks and how to waterproof EVERYTHING! Pararescuemen will be introduced to the "tree suit," officially called the Parachutist Rough Terrain System, or PRTS. This is a specially manufactured suit having extra padding to protect the neck, armpits, kidneys, elbows, crotch, and knees of the jumper. It was designed for the purpose of jumping into heavily wooded environments and has a large pocket to stow up to 50 feet of rope to facilitate lowering the jumper to the ground should the parachutist get hung up in a tree. Each trainee will make 10 land jumps, 2 tree jumps, and 5 SCUBA jumps, totaling 17, of which 4 to 6 will be night jumps.

Upon completion of this course, the qualified airman is ready for assignment to any pararescue unit worldwide. Those who complete the pararescue training are awarded the maroon beret and wear the Air Force crest, "That Others May Live."

Combat Controller Path

The combat control direction takes on the following challenges. The first stop is Keesler Air Force Base, Mississippi, for the Combat Control Operator Course, lasting 15 1/2 weeks. The candidate will be under the instruction of both civilian and U.S. Air Force air traffic controllers. This course teaches orientation into air traffic control and basic flight rules, VFR tower, radar approach control (RAPCON) procedures, aircraft recognition, aircraft performance, air navigational aids, weather, airport traffic control, flight assistance, communications, conventional approach control, and air traffic control. This is the meat and potatoes of the combat controller's task. Combat controller trainees also attend a five-day combat nonradar class. At the conclusion of this course they are prepared to take the Federal Aviation Administration's Control Tower Operator examination.

The final class that separates the CCTs from the PJs is the Combat Control School, at Pope Air

Technical Sergeant Dirk Wenrich, PJ in the IFAM cadre, prepares a "crash" victim for a training exercise. Once this casualty has been moulaged up, the sergeant will apply generous amounts of goop to simulate major lacerations. The PJ will have to locate the wounded aircrewman and determine the extent of his injuries, often merely by the color of the blood. For example, when the goop is more pinkish, it would indicate a lung injury.

Force Base, North Carolina, Master Sergeant Paul Venturella, an instructor at the Combat Control School, relates the school's mission as, "To train United States Air Force and select joint and allied service personnel basic combat skills to support controlling air traffic in an austere combat airhead operation, [and] to provide specialized advance skills training to support combat control team leader duties, static line Jumpmaster duties, and survey operations." For the next 12 weeks and 3 days the school's cadre will carry out this mission with their students. Class size varies; 11 trainees per class is the average, with an optimum of 20. The course includes combat tactics, communication and navigational equipment, land navigation, assault zone operations, air traffic control, demolitions, fire support, and concludes with a field training exercise.

As with all branches of the service, when you hit a new school or base you go through the in-processing. For the candidates arriving at the Combat Control School it is no different. Here they are checked out in various procedures, such as CPR (cardiopulmonary resuscitation). They are issued their equipment and, like their pararescue teammates, they receive the standard ALICE field pack, size large. Unlike the PJs' medical rucksack, MSgt. Venturella explains, "The thing about CCT is we do so many types of missions in many different manners and configurations that it's almost impossible to list a 'standard' load." The mission dictates what the CCT will pack, he continues. "I've been on numerous real-world and training missions with rucks that can weigh as little as 30 pounds and as much as 110 pounds."

If the mission was going to be primarily air traffic control then the controller would carry the appropriate radio setup. Along with the radio he would carry the necessary antennas, accouterments, and extra batteries. If the team is going in to set up a runway or landing zone, they would distribute the equipment among the team. Some would carry the radios, while others would pack lights, batteries, recognition panels and stakes to make the runway. In addition to this equipment, the CCT might include various types of electronic navigational aids, a light-gun, NVGs, or a weather kit. While certain missions do indeed determine the type of equipment, there are three items that I have never seen a CCT member without: a radio, a strobe with IR cover, and a weapon.

While at the CCT school, physical conditioning is continuously stressed. Physical training is conducted throughout the 87 days of training. One day the student may be doing a 6-mile run; the next day will find him performing pool work or weight training, with a rucksack march rounding out the week. This constant physical preparation ensures that future combat controllers will be up to the task, both physically and mentally for the course, field training exercise, and their assignment to a Special Tactics Squadron.

"PJ Forward!" The call goes out and the STS pararescueman proceeds toward a downed C-130. Note he is carrying an HK MP5, AN/PRC126 interteam radio and special medical ruck. Once aboard the aircraft the PJ will assess the injured and communicate their status to the senior PJ at the collection point.

The first two weeks of training is in tactics. In this block, the instructors impart their knowledge in small unit tactics. Students will become familiar with various weapons that will be carried on their missions. Methods of insertion from rappelling to fast roping will be taught. Team leader procedures, field hygiene, gas mask (NBC) methods, and field craft are all included in this block. At the end of the twelve weeks the students perform a tactical, static-line parachute jump for an overnight FTX that will apply the skills learned in this block.

The next block of training is communications/navigational equipment. One of the most important tools employed by a CCT is his radio. Here the CCT will learn the practical applications that will be used in his assignment to an STS as a combat controller: radio equipment that allows ground-to-air and ground-to-ground communications; radios, such as the PRC-117D, that are useful to talk on all the radio nets (networks or frequencies), VHF, AM/FM, UHF AM/FM and SATCOM, except HF; portable radios;

interteam radios; and radios mounted inside Humvees. Concurrently, communication security (COMSEC) and command and control communication will be covered in this block.

While communication is an essential tool of a CCT, it is not of much use if the aircraft has nowhere to land, or the helo has no LZ. In addition to the plethora of radio equipment, the students are exposed to a vast array of navigational aids and equipment. They will be taught how to employ the B-2 Light gun; how to set up a runway with as little as five lights, a technique know as "Box and One"; how to use cloth panel markers, known as VS-17 panels; and how to use strobes, normal issue with IR covers to small programmable units the size of 9-volt batteries. Instruction is given on how to set up landing lights, colored as well as IR. These lights can all be controlled from a small hand unit similar to a TV remote. A practical test using all the equipment is given at the end of the class.

There will be times when the CCTs jump in with the assault force. Other times they will have to jump in with other SOFs or perhaps on their own to perform an SR or RST. On these occasions they will use the information obtained in the land navigation block at the CCT school, starting off with the basics, practical work with a map and compass, and use of the military grid reference system (MGRS). Once comfortable with these methods, they move on to GPS procedures and point-to-point navigation. As with the previous blocks, it ends with a three-day FTX to evaluate the student's land navigation skills.

In the assault zone block they will receive practical training in the basics of establishing a drop zone, landing zone, and helicopter landing zone (HLZ). Using visual aids, they will learn how to marshal aircraft once on the ground and perform limited weather observations and assault zone management. This culminates in the establishment of an assault zone and block test.

Upon hitting the ground the CCT may be required to remove obstacles from the tarmac to allow follow-on forces to land uninhibited. For this reason the students go through the demolitions block. For five days they will receive knowledge and practical instruction: how to safely employ nonelectric demolitions. Nonelectric is defined as a timed fuse method, as opposed to command detonation. Demolition techniques will be taught, including the Saddle Charge, used to cut cylindrical, mild steel targets up to 8 inches in diameter; Diamond Charge, used to cut either mild or alloy cylindrical steel of any diameter; Ribbon Charge, used to cut noncylindrical steel, that is, I beams, angle irons, and so on, up to 2 inches thick; and others. This culminates in practical testing in the applications, calculations, and placement of explosives.

The last block of instruction at Pope Air Force Base is fire support for four days. In the communication block the student learns how to use the radio as a tool. In this block he discovers how to transform the radio into a weapon called close air sup-

Working together, a Ranger pitches in to assist the STS pararescuemen as they tend to an injured crewmember. The PJs of AFSOC are among the highest-trained medical specialists in SOCOM. While their mission is to aid the injured, they are combatants and keep their weapons, a M-4 and MP5, close at hand.

Combat Controller Staff Sergeant Rick Driggers listens to the pilot of "Cowboy Zero-3," an incoming Pave Low that will provide CAS to his STS team. SSgt. Drigger wears the IBH, integrated ballistic helmet. This helmet is being evaluated as a replacement for the Gentex helmets now in use. The IBH is a Kevlar helmet with communications gear attached to the headgear.

port, or CAS. Training consists of integrating CAS with ground- and sea-based weapons systems, night operations, laser procedures, mission execution, and how to call for fire interfacing with AC-130 gunships and helicopters for CAS. You only have to spend a few moments on Alpha 77 at Eglin Air Force Base to realize the awesome effect of CAS. As with the other blocks, it ends with practical evaluation of skills learned.

Now that our future combat controllers have been schooled in their trade, they are off to the Sand Hills of North Carolina, just west of Camp McKall, where the Army SF has its Q-course and SERE school. They will spend the next 10 days in a comprehensive FTX applying all of the skills taught over the past 12 weeks. It begins with a mission plan, team leader brief, and equipment preparation. When they are "good to go" they will be inserted into their assigned area of operations (AO). After insertion, the students will receive various follow-on missions for the next eight days. They will be required to plan, prepare, and rehearse each mission prior to its execution. The FTX mission includes the establishment of numerous assault zones; FRIS insertion and HLZ; a run through the obstacle course (Q-course at SF Camp McKall); patrol base operations; movement of the team overland, perhaps an SR; practical exercise (equipment and procedures); and CAS knowledge employing lasing procedures using a laser designator referred to as the SOFLAM or Special Operation Force Laser Acquisition Marker. The final mission includes a border crossing back into friendly territory. On the final morning of the FTX is a 15-mile rucksack march from the field to the Combat Control School. Students are required to carry 70 pounds in their rucksack, LBE, and weapon.

Those airmen and officers completing this phase of training are qualified for assignment as combat controllers. Some will be assigned to conventional CCT in Air Combat Command, while those entering AFSOC will be assigned to one of the four Special Tactics Squadrons in the continental United States. It is at the end of this course that they are awarded the scarlet beret, with the Air Force crest, "First There."

For the STS team member, this is just the beginning. They will go on to receive intense training in deploying the special air asset of AFSOC, including advanced training in working with "fast movers" for CAS and become Special Operations Tactical Air Control (SOTAC) qualified. They will undergo Ranger training and other "infantry"-related skills.

All of the training of the "pipeline" is essential to the success of the STS mission. It is not that they will be given the assignment to take an airfield; that would go to the Rangers. They would not be asked to fast rope onto a building and perform a hostage rescue; these operations are tasked to the SEALs or DELTA Force. In each scenario, however, there will be air assets involved and possible casualties. The STS teams will be there to support such operations. This is the reason for the intensity of the "pipeline" and subsequent training. When a member of an STS team is attached to other SOF units, they must be an asset, not a liability. "The last thing you want to do is slow that SEAL team down." Master Sergeant Ron Childress (ret.) explains, "If you do . . . they will not call you in again."

Special Tactics—Initial Familiarization (IFAM)

Initial Familiarization, or IFAM, is the gathering of PJs and CCT into a cohesive unit where they are exposed to all the aspects, methods, and procedures carried out in STS operations. It is an exercise that will mold these airmen into the lethal force known as air commandos; it lasts one month!

During IFAM the PJs and CCTs, both "rookies" and experienced, will run through the paces of the "bread and butter" of STS. Childress, a combat veteran CCT, coordinates the sessions. "Here they [STS teams] find out exactly WHAT we do and HOW we do it," Childress said. He and the IFAM cadre impart their knowledge, lessons learned, experience, and motivation into the up-and-coming teams that will take their place in the Special Tactics Squadrons.

IFAM begins with an introduction of Special Tactics, a USSCOM briefing, and a history of STS. For the next 30 days the STS teams will transition from classroom lectures on airfield seizure to the expanses of Eglin Air Force Base to carry out what they learned, then it's back to the team room for a debrief, call it a day, then start all over tomorrow with aircraft familiarization, then out to the tarmac to run

through a Spectre or a Pave Low. Here the crews will instruct them on the aircraft's capabilities and weapons systems.

The STS team members will work with GPS and with radios, then be transported out to the swamps of Eglin, where they will navigate their Zodiac rafts through the Yellow River, home to the 6th Ranger Training Brigade, as well as numerous alligators and a few cottonmouths. (None of which you want to meet on a dark night.)

They will learn how to rig a Zodiac for a "rubber duck" mission, the K-Duck, T-Duck, Double Duck, Hard and Soft Ducks, and the rigid alternate method Zodiac (RAMZ). Once this is done, it's over to Duke Air Force Base where they will suit up, load up on a Combat Shadow, and head out to deploy the Zodiac package and parachute down after it. They will hit the water, inflate the raft, and ride it in for the next phase of the mission.

After an orientation on the motorcycles, quads, and RATT by an STS sergeant who treats these vehicles like a hen caring for her chicks, they grab a bite to eat, no MREs for them (remember this is the Air Force). Later in the evening, they will load these various modes of transportation onto a Combat Talon. This exercise will acquaint them with rapid ON/OFF loading techniques. The term explains the procedure: You get off and you get on fast!

The MC-130H will taxi to position, lower its ramp, and the STS will speed off onto the runway, perform a foreign object and debris search, then quickly load up on the Talon again. The Talon will take off, circle the field, land, and the STS will go through the routine again and again, until this becomes second nature to them. By the way, this is all taking place at "oh-dark thirty" with the use of NVGs.

The whole time IFAM is progressing the PJs and CCTs are each honing their skills. PJs will perform triage at a simulated crash site. Prior to arriving at the location of the "downed" C-130, the IFAM cadre has been hard at work preparing the plane and casualties for the pararescuemen. IFAM Technical Sergeant

Dirk Wenrich carries in a large case and sets it on the deck of the C-130.

Upon opening the moulage kit, one may think that the sergeant is a Hollywood special effects expert getting ready for the next horror show. In a way he is. The kit contains latex appliques of all sorts of nasty things that one hopes never happens to them (i.e., spilled intestines, lacerations with exposed bone, and assorted other rubber "injuries"). He picks out one, then another, and applies the simulated wounds to the volunteer aircrewman. He then picks up a bottle of "goop" that is a special concoction of gelatin, glycerin, and red food coloring, which he generously pours on the wounds to simulate blood.

With the wounded man all "made up," the sergeant puts him in position for the PJs to locate and treat. Before the PJs get to the plane, however, he fires up a smoke generator and the fuselage fills with thick gray-white smoke. Now we're ready.

While the PJs enact the rescue, the CCTs are on the radios engaged in the job of managing the air assets. This is an extremely important task. First, it is comforting to know that you have an AC-130 gunship orbiting overhead ready to answer a "call for fire." Second, you may have a Pave Low coming in to deliver more Rangers or the REDS gear for the PJs. Third, that Pave Low is your ride home. The last thing you want to have happen is for the MH-53 to be flying in as the Spectre is impacting the AO with 105-millimeter rounds, or the "fast movers" (jets) are beginning their bomb run.

Precise management of your air space is essential to your wounded, to the air crews, to the mission, and, finally, to yourself. It is times like this that the CCT is worth his weight in gold and is exactly the reason that they train constantly. Staff Sergeant Rick Driggers, IFAM CCT, explains, "You want that helicopter there when it's time to get out of Dodge."

Further exercises will include establishment of an FARRP, or Forward Area Refueling and Re-arming Point; marshaling aircraft; techniques for survey of a DZ, LZ, and HLZ; weapons familiarization (pistols,

rifles, submachine guns, M-60s, and sniper rifles); and helicopter operations in urban areas, wooded areas, and helo-casting. The IFAM attendees will have more than a few times to experience fast roping out of a Pave Low. Then, upon mission's end, CCTs will climb back up via a rope ladder. On and on it goes, instilling the skills that transform a trooper into an air commando.

All of this training and practicing is in preparation for the final mission. The STS teams formed in the IFAM will be attached to a Ranger unit. Together with the "shooters" they will plan, rehearse, and execute an airfield seizure.

Upon the culmination of IFAM are graduation day and the Monster Mash, a huge party carried out on the beaches of the Gulf of Mexico, across the intercoastal waterway from Hurlburt Field. Here the graduates and other invitees celebrate their completion of this phase of training. To the uninformed, the activities of the Mash might appear to be an extension of the field exercises. During the celebrations, the STS team will shoulder a Zodiac and run over the sand dunes in a race to the Gulf. All of the activities and merriment serve to bond the graduates into a team of warriors, where they will depend on each other, not only for the success of their mission, but for survival itself. All in a day's work for the Quiet Professionals of AFSOC's Special Tactics Squadron.

10th Combat Weather Squadron

Assigned to the 720th Special Tactics Squadron, is the 10th Combat Weather Squadron. Its mission is to provide meteorological and oceanographic information in and for the special operations theater of operations. Their functions include tactical infiltration, data collection, analysis and forecasting, mission tailoring of environmental data, and operating jointly with a host nation's weather personnel. CWS personnel perform this job from a forward-deployed base or at times from behind enemy lines using tactical weather equipment and an assortment of communications equipment.

A combat weatherman calls in weather data he has gathered. Such information as wind velocity and barometric readings will aid in decision making for theater commanders. Although assigned to AFSOC, they do not go through the pipeline as do the STS troops.

CWS operates with subordinate units of the U.S. Army's Special Operations Command (USASOC), Special Forces Command (USASFC), and Civil Affairs/Psychological Operations Command (USACAPOC). The CWS trains and maintains readiness of assigned forces to conduct special combat operations anytime, anywhere, independently, or attached to USASOC units.

The Combat Weather Squadron can trace its lineage to air and ground combat and Special Operations since 1943. One of the earliest commanders of the squadron was Lieutenant Colonel (later Brigadier General) Richard Ellsworth. He and the 10th WS operated with Colonel Phillip Cochran's 1st Air Commando Group, Brigadier Orde Wingates Chindit's (long-range penetration teams) and Brigadier General Frank Merrill's 5037th Composite Infantry Provisional ("Merrill's Marauder"). The nature of weather on operations in the China-Burma-India Theater demanded the use of small weather teams inserted to provide observations from deep within enemy territory.

In June 1966 the 10th WS was reactivated at Udorn Airfield, Thailand, to conduct combat weather operations in Southeast Asia. The squadron also trained indigenous personnel and set up clandestine weather observation networks throughout the region. Tenth Weather Squadron personnel were key players in many successful special operations, including the Son Tay raid, America's attempt to rescue POWs from a prison camp in North Vietnam. Timing for the "raid" was advanced by 24 hours based on the forecast done by 10th WS.

On 1 April 1996, the 10th Weather Squadron was redesignated the 10th Combat Weather Squadron (10th CWS) at Fort Bragg, North Carolina. This one squadron is comprised of five detachments located within the United States and two separate overseas operating locations. Special operation forces supported by the 10th CWS include U.S. Army Special Forces, U.S. Army Rangers, 160th Special Operations Aviation Regiment, Psychological Operations Group, Special Warfare Training Groups, Civil Affairs units, and Special Operations Support Battalions.

Although assigned to AFSOC, they do not go through the pipeline, as do the STS troops.

Chapter 6

Special Operations Techniques

There are times when a team cannot just drop into an enemy's back yard, for political reasons, or strategic or tactical considerations. You must insert your team clandestinely from afar and outside of the nation's territorial airspace or boundaries. For such an insertion a U.S. Special Operations team would use either High Altitude Low Opening (HALO) or High Altitude High Opening (HAHO). Both of these methods are common among U.S. Navy SEALs and U.S. Army Special Forces A-teams. For that reason, the AFSOC STS teams will also learn and become proficient in performing these procedures alongside their Army and Navy SOF operators.

These types of parachute operations will be flights over or adjacent to the objective area from altitudes not normally associated with conventional static-line parachuting. HALO/HAHO infiltrations are normally conducted under the cover of darkness or at twilight to lessen the chance of observation by hostile forces. Using the RAPS, the STS teams deploy their parachutes at a designated altitude, assemble in the air, and land together in the arranged drop zone to begin their mission. This type of drop can be conducted even in adverse weather conditions.

Flying at an altitude of 25,000 to 43,000 feet MSL (mean sea level), a Combat Talon will appear as legitimate aircraft on an enemy's radar screen, perhaps just another commercial airliner traversing the globe. What the radar operator will not know is that the aircraft is the launching platform for the world's most lethal system, a detachment of highly trained U.S. Army Special Forces, "shooters" with their assigned STS team attached.

Military free fall operations (MFF) are ideally adapted for the infiltration of STS and SOF personnel. While the maximum exit altitude is 43,000 feet MSL, MFF operations may be as low as 5,000 feet above ground level (AGL). A typical STS team can be deployed in the fraction of the time it would take a conventional static-line jump. Normal opening altitudes range from 3,500 AGL to 25,000 MSL, depending on mission parameters.

As the AFSOC pilots approach the insertion point, the ramp of the MC-130H will lower. With the combination of aircraft noise and wearing the MFF parachutist helmet and oxygen mask, any type of verbal communication is almost impossible. For this reason the team will communicate with arm-and-hand signals. Having already received the signals to don helmets, unfasten seat belts, and check oxygen, the jumpmaster waits for the team to signal back "OK." Further instruction will be given to the jumpers as to wind speed and any gusting, all using silent signaling.

Approximately two minutes before the insertion, the jumpmaster raises his arm upward from his side indicating the team should "stand up." Next he extends his arm straight out at shoulder level, palm up, then bends it to touch his helmet, this indicating "move to the rear." The Special Tactics Team members, equipped with ram-air parachutes, oxygen masks, and goggles, stand up and get ready to jump. If jumping from the side jump door, he'll be a meter away; if going out the rear of the plane, the lead man will stop at the hinge of the cargo ramp. With their rucksacks filled with mission-essential equipment,

High altitude low opening (HALO) and high altitude high opening (HAHO) are two methods commonly practiced by U.S. special operation forces. Members of the Special Tactics Squadrons are proficient in their use and fully capable of clandestine insertion with Army or Navy Special Forces.

An STS Combat Controller fast ropes out of a MH-53E. For this trip, his team will exit the starboard door of the helicopter. The fast rope may also be attached in the rear of the aircraft and the special operations troops would exit off the rear cargo ramp. The proper procedure is to swing out so your rucksack does not get caught on the airframe and hang you up. This CCT member is properly positioned and on his way to a fast slide to the ground. Carrying an AN/PRC 117 radio, he will be ready to set up for close air support upon hitting the ground. Once the team has completed the fast rope, the rope may be dropped or dragged back into the helicopter so no telltale signs are left of the STT insertion.

they waddle toward the rear of the plane. Moments turn into an eternity, and then it is time; as the aircraft reaches the proper coordinates for the drop, the jump light emits a steady green. The command is given, "Go!" In a matter of seconds the team of Air Commandos, looking like a giant centipede, shuffles down the ramp and out into the darkness as the drone of the plane's engines fades off in the distance.

Depending on the mission parameters, they will perform a HALO or HAHO jump. In HALO, the team will exit the plan and free fall through the airspace, meeting up at a prearranged time or altitude. Jumping in this manner, the team is so small that they are virtually invisible and, of course, will not show up on any enemy radar screen. Using GPS units and altimeters, the team will descend until fairly close to the drop zone. At that point they will open their chutes and prepare for the very short trip to the ground.

The alternate method HAHO is also jumping from an extreme height with oxygen. The difference is that as soon as the team jumps off, they immediately deploy their parachutes and use them to glide into a denied area. For this type of jump, they would also use GPS units and altimeters. To maintain formation integrity, each jumper would have a strobe on his helmet, either normal or IR, and the team would wear the appropriate NVGs. Additionally, each team member would be on interteam radio for command and control of the insertion, as well as formation on the DZ.

There are a number of advantages of using the HALO/HAHO procedures. There are times when the presence of enemy air defenses makes it best to infiltrate a team into a hostile area. This also increases the survivability of the support aircraft. If the mission requires the team to jump into a mountainous terrain where it would not be practical or prudent to attempt a static-line parachute operation, MFF would be a practical option. Other benefits include times when navigational aids (NAVAIDS) are not available to guarantee the requisite precision of drops at low altitudes (i.e., deserts or jungle environments), or when it is deemed necessary to land the team at multiple points of an objective for the purpose of attacking or seizing a primary target and the mission success requires a low-signature infiltration.

FRIS

The fast rope insertion system (FRIS) is the new way to get your assault force on the ground in seconds. This system begins with small, woven wool ropes that are braided into a larger rope. The rope is rolled into a deployment bag and the end is secured to the helicopter. Depending on the model of chopper, it can be just outside on the hoist mechanism or attached to a bracket off the back ramp. Once over the insertion point the rope is deployed, and even as it is hitting the ground the STS team members are jumping onto it and sliding down, as easily as a firefighter goes down a pole. Once the team is safely on the ground, the gunner or flight engineer on the helicopter will pull the safety pin, and the rope will fall to the ground. Such a system is extremely useful in the rapid deployment of Special Tactics Squadrons personnel, as well as the other special operation forces that have mastered the technique. Unlike rappelling, once the trooper hits the ground, he is "free" of the rope and can begin his mission.

SPIES

While fast-roping gets you down quick, there are times when you have to get out of Dodge just as fast. The problem is, there is no LZ for the MH-53E Pave Low to land, and the bad guys are closing in on your position. This technique began during the Vietnam War as the McGuire rig, then it was modified to the STABO rig. Both used multiple ropes, which often resulted in the troops colliding into one another; the latter at least had the benefit of allowing the user to use his weapon while on the ride up. What served the Special Forces troops of the sixties has been refined to the new Special Procedure Insertion Extraction System (SPIES) method.

When it is time to extract and there is no HLZ available, the STT may employ SPIES (special procedure insertion/extraction system). Unlike the old STABO technique, which would only accommodate four men, SPIES will allow up to eight men "on the wire" at one time. Wearing a special harness, this snap link is attached to a rope that is deployed from a hovering helicopter. Once out of harm's way, the pilot will find a safe place to land, and the team will climb inside the helicopter.

While the technique has changed, the methodology remains. A *single* rope is lowered from the hovering helicopter. Attached to this rope are rings, woven and secured into the rope at approximately 5 feet intervals. There can be as many as eight rings on the rope. The STS team members, wearing special

A Double Duck. Two fully inflated Zodiac rafts are palletized, rigged, and await loading onto an AFSOC aircraft. Among the load will be the engines that will be installed once they hit the water. After the Double Duck is quickly assembled, the STT will enter the raft and begin their overwater insertion.

harnesses similar to parachute harnesses, will attach themselves to the rope, via the rings. This is accomplished by clipping in a snap link that is at the top of the harness.

Once all team members are secured, a signal is given and the STS team becomes airborne in reverse and extracted out of harm's way. While tried and tested, this method allows the team to maintain covering fire from their weapons as they extract.

Once the STS team has been rushed out of enemy range and an LZ can be located, the helicopter pilot will bring the troops to ground again. At this time they will disconnect from the rope and board the chopper, which will then finish the extraction.

SPIES is not without risks, as the pilot of the helicopter must take care not to drag the commandos through the trees or other permanent ground fixtures, such as rocks, mountain sides, or buildings. The AFSOC helicopter pilots are remarkably proficient at seeing this does not happen.

Rappelling

With Fast Rope Insertion System (FRIS) being the most accepted way of getting a force onto the ground expeditiously, there are still occasions when STS teams will use rappelling to accomplish their mission. There are times when working in a mountainous terrain, or in an urban environment, that this technique will come in handy.

Attaching regular military-issue rope through carabiners, or a specially designed rappelling device (known as a "Figure 8"), the team will negotiate down the side of a mountain to reach a downed pilot or establish an observation point for SR.

This old mountaineering technique has served Special Forces troops for decades and is still a viable asset in the inventory of skills of the Special Tactics Squadrons.

Rubber Duck

A *rubber duck* is the term SOF troops will use to describe a mission where there is a need to deploy a Zodiac raft. There are numerous methods of conveying the craft to the water, and the AFSOC aircrews and STS teams are specialists at all of them.

There is the *Soft Duck*. Here the fully inflated Zodiac raft is deployed from the rear cargo ramp of a MH-53 Pave Low or a MH-47 Chinook. The raft is slid out of the helicopter and the STT follows right behind. Once in the water, the team jumps in, fires up the outboard engine, and heads out on the mission. An alternate to this is the *Hard Duck*; this is a craft with a metal bottom, and it is delivered in the same manner as the Soft Duck.

Another method of deployment is the K Duck; the K stands for *kangaroo*. As the name implies, the Zodiac raft is slung underneath a Pave Hawk. It is fully inflated and mission ready upon hitting the water. Rounding out the alphabet ducks is the *T Duck; T* stands for *tether*. In this case the raft is totally deflated, rolled up, and secured inside the helicopter. Once deployed, as before, the team will inflate, load up, and begin its mission.

Moving from the rotary to the fixed-wing methods, there is the *RAMZ* drop. Pronounced "rams," it is defined as a Rigging Alternate

The STS members are capable of inserting by land, air, and, in this case, sea. As this scout swimmer of the STT arrives on the beach, he'll pause at the water's edge. Keeping his rifle up and ready he will survey the surroundings, ready to bring the rest of the team up on his signal.

Method–Zodiac. Originally designed by the PJs for NASA shuttle missions, the Zodiac raft is fully deflated and secured to a disposable pallet; parachutes are then attached to the harness, securing the package. Moments after the loadmaster releases the package, the STS troops will shuffle to the end of the ramp and parachute in after it. A variation of the deflated method is the *Double Duck*, where two Zodiacs, fully inflated, are stacked and deployed via parachute together. Both the RAMZ and Double would be delivered by a Combat Talon or Combat Shadow.

105

In 1985, the United States military adopted the Beretta Model 92F 9-millimeter semiautomatic pistol as the standard-issue sidearm for U.S. troops. Designated the M9, this 9-millimeter handgun began to replace the aging 1911 pistols in an effort to standardize the 9-millimeter NATO ammunition.

Along with the standardization of the 9-millimeter, the M9 brought the armed forces a larger-capacity magazine. The M9 holds 15 rounds compared to the Colt 1911's 7 or 8 rounds. Although the 9-millimeter ammunition was lighter and smaller, it was viewed that this was adequate for line troops. This trade-off also allowed the troops to engage more rounds in a firefight before needing to reload.

The original M9s were viewed with some apprehension among operators in the Special Operations community when the usage of +P ammunition reportedly caused stress fractures of the M9 slides. Beretta addressed this problem, and today's M9 has an average life of 72,250 rounds.

The M9 has seen service with U.S. troops, both conventional and special, in Operation Urgent Fury in Grenada, Operation Desert Shield and Storm in Kuwait, Operation Restore Hope in Somalia, and IFOR in Bosnia.

The M9 features a rotating firing pin system with decocking and trigger bar disconnect. A magazine release is positioned at the base of the trigger guard, accommodating either left-handed or right-handed shooters.

The rescue all-terrain transport (RATT) is at home in the woods as well as on the tarmac. Here two PJs maneuver through the brush to search for wounded in this secluded HLZ. A combat controller, armed with a HK MP5, rides shotgun.

Another feature unique to the M9 is the fact that when there is a round in the chamber, the extractor head angles out to function as a "loaded" indicator. In the daylight it can be easily seen by its red tip, while at night it can be felt. The ambidextrous safety lever features a triple safety. When the safety lever is pushed on, three safety features are activated. The striker is rotated out of alignment, the hammer is decocked, and the trigger bar is disconnected from the hammer/sear mechanism.

The slide is open for nearly the entire length of the barrel. This facilitates the ejection of spent shells and virtually eliminates stoppages. The open slide configuration also provides a means for the pistol to be loaded manually.

As with all weapons in use with special operation forces, the operators are always trying to get that extra edge. One of the most likely features to be added to the M9 was a sound suppressor. For such a device the military turned to Knight Armament Company to produce the needed suppresser. The smooth, cylindrical suppresser is made of anodized aluminum with a steel attachment system. Weighing a scant 6 ounces, it can be replaced or removed in three seconds. Carrying over the Vietnam-era name, the suppressor was dubbed the "Hush-Puppy."

M9 Specifications:

Caliber: 9-millimeter NATO; **weight:** (empty magazine) 2.2 pounds; **capacity:** 15 + 1; **length:** 8.5 inches, 13.75 inches (with suppressor); **barrel length:** 4.92 inches.

HK Mk 23 Model 0—SOCOM Pistol

There have been volumes written on the differences between 9-millimeter and .45-caliber munitions and

The Heckler and Koch MP5 9-millimeter submachine gun is the weapon of choice for many special operation forces, especially for close-quarters battle (CQB). As a member of the Blue Team of the 720th STS states, "HK-the easy way out!"

A suppressed Berretta, which uses the NATO 9-millimeter round.

handguns. We will not add to this debate here. In fact, Delta Force never adopted the 9-millimeter and opted to stay with the .45. Suffice it to say that when it comes to handguns, special operation operators always come back to their first love, the .45-caliber.

In August 1991, Heckler and Koch Inc. and Colt Manufacturing Company were awarded contracts to develop an offensive handgun weapon system (OHWS) by the USSOCOM. The OHWS consists of three components: (1) a .45-caliber pistol, (2) a laser-aiming module, and (3) a sound and flash suppressor.

Divided into three phases for development and testing, SOCOM was to select one of the two pistol systems by the end of Phase II. In August 1992, both companies had delivered 30 prototypes to the U.S. Navy for evaluation and extensive testing. Cost proposals went out for Phases II and III in October 1993.

In January 1994, the OHWS developed by Heckler and Koch was selected and a Phase II contract was awarded. HK GmbH of Oberndorf, Germany, continued work on the pistol while development of the suppressor was done by Knight Armament Company, Florida, and the laser-aiming

module (LAM) went to Insight Technologies Inc. (ITI) of New Hampshire.

In November 1994 30 preproduction .45s with suppressors were delivered for further testing and evaluation. Testing was to be completed around April 1995 with a Phase III production contract scheduled for no later that July 1995.

The Special Operation Forces Offensive Handgun, as it is now referred to, was put through some of the most stringent operational requirements ever demanded. Tests would require the HK weapon to deliver a minimum of 2,000 mean rounds between stoppages (MRBS) with both M1911 ball and +P ammunition. During testing, the MRBS was 6,027 with a maximum of 15,122.

In more than 450 accuracy tests, the prototype pistols far exceeded government requirements with 65 groups of less than 1 inch. There were four 1/2-inch groups, with five rounds going through the same hole. This evaluation was done with and without the sound suppressor attached.

To meet operational environmental requirements, the pistol was tested at +160 and -60 degrees F, exposed to two hours of sea water at 66 feet, and in surf, sand, mud, icing, and unlubricated. A special maritime surface coating protected the pistol from any corrosion in all of these environments.

Stealth and secrecy can best be maintained with the help of a sound-suppressed weapon. Here we see the newly issued HK Mark 23 Model 0 SOCOM pistol, with sound suppresser and LAM. Though much longer than the older 1911-style .45-caliber pistols, this handgun is deadly accurate. The suppressor can actually be fine-tuned to change the grouping of rounds on target. The LAM or laser aiming module has a white light, IR, and laser sight.

The HK MK23 pistol has an effective recoil-reduction system that reduces recoil forces to the components and shooter by 40 percent. It is a double/single-action pistol with a 12-round-capacity magazine. The barrel is threaded to accept attachments such as the KAC sound suppressor, and the frame is grooved to accept the ITI LAM. The weapon is aimed by a three-dot white of self-luminous tritium dots, or the LAM.

Another unique feature of the MK23 is the decocking lever. This allows the hammer to be lowered quietly, which can prove to be quite beneficial on a covert operation when there are "bad guys" around. When the hammer is down the safety lever is blocked in the fire positions so that the pistol is always ready for double-action operation. When the hammer if cocked and the safety set to "safe," the decocker is blocked so that the pistol is ready for single-action operation, by moving the safety to the "fire" position. The extended slide relapse and ambidextrous magazine release are easily actuated without adjustment of the firing grip.

The Colt M-4 is similar to the CAR-15 developed during the Vietnam era. The M-4 incorporates semi-automatic or full-automatic fire selection. This carbine version of the M-16A1 is fitted with the M-203 40-millimeter grenade launcher.

LAM

The LAM is the result of more than four years of development by Insight Technology, USSOCOM, and the Naval Surface Warfare Center, Crane Division. The LAM contains visible and infrared lasers for aiming, infrared illuminator, and a visible white light.

Simple to operate and offering a wide range of capabilities not available with any other night vision device of its size, the current-model LAM is designed to be securely attached to the MK23 using the mounting grooves on the frame of the weapon.

Attachment of the LAM does not affect the functionality of the weapon, and the unit can be detached and reattached to the pistol while maintaining a repeatable bore-sight of better than .4 inches at 25 meters.

The LAM can operate in one of four selected operational modes. This is accomplished by rotating the selector switch of the side of the LAM to the desired position. The four modes of operation are:

- Visible laser only
- Visible laser/flashlight
- Infrared laser only
- Infrared laser/illuminator

Once the mode has been selected, the LAM is easily activated in either a momentary or steady-on condition by depressing a switch lever located just forward of the pistol's trigger guard. Internal bore-sight adjusters allow the LAM to be precisely zeroed to the weapon.

The current-issue sound suppressor deployed by USSOCOM for the HK MK23 pistol is the .45 Cal Suppressor manufactured by Knight Armament Company. One of the unique features of this suppressor is the fact that the operator may loosen and indexed [note: do you mean to say that it is indexed to ten different positions?] to ten different positions. This allows the operator to adjust the weapon's point of impact within 2 inches. Constructed of stainless steel, the suppressor is welded to five baffles (star-shaped sections). Weighing 1 pound, the KAC suppressor can be attached or removed to the MK23 in a matter of seconds. It requires very low maintenance and has an extremely long life. Decibels reduction is rated at 38 decibels (wet) or 28 decibels (dry). SOF operators report that with the suppressor on all you hear is the sound of the action.

Specifications:

Caliber: 45 ACP; **weight:** 3.22 pounds (with loaded magazine), 4.22 pounds (with suppressor); **capacity:** 12 + 1 staggered; **length:** 9.65 inches, 16.56 inches (with suppressor); **barrel length:** 5.875 inches.

HK MP5 Series

There are instances when mission parameters dictate that the M16 variants are left in the armory and the HK submachine guns come out. Close quarter battle (CQB) might call for the MP5, and when stealth and secrecy are priorities the Special Forces community goes in armed with MP5 SD3s (a suppressed version).

The MP5 is simple to handle as well as fast and accurate, whether firing from the shoulder or the hip. Its high accuracy results from the fixed barrel, which is cold forged with the cartridge chamber. The recoil of the MP5s is extremely

There are times when you need to enter with only a whisper. For those occasions, the STT will use the MP5-SD3. This is the same type of submachine gun as the MP5, but is fitted with an integral sound suppressor. The most noise comes from the action of the bolt as it chambers and ejects 9-millimeter rounds. Pictured is one propped up against an integrated ballistics helmet and fitted with an assault sling.

smooth, allowing the STS trooper to obtain highly accurate shot placement.

It fires a 9-millimeter Parabellum pistol round usually carried in a 30-round magazine, often equipped with a dual magazine holder. An operator with an MP5 can be very effective in clearing an enemy control tower or other mission-critical target.

The MP5 family of submachine guns are automatic weapons, firing from a closed bolt. Modes of fire are sustained (firing automatic as long as the trigger is held back), semi-automatic (single shot each time the trigger is pulled), and three-round burst. All MP5 versions have identical subassembles, ensuring that many of the components of the various weapons are interchangeable within the HK weapon system.

A Special Forces captain was once asked what weapon he would choose if he could choose just one to take on a mission. Without hesitation he answered, "the HK MP5." He is not alone in his accolades of the HK weapon systems. You will find these submachine guns in the inventories of U.S. Navy SEALs , U.S. Army Delta Force, and the British SAS. Enough said.

There may be times when an STS needs to neutralize an enemy from a distance. The SR-25 fitted with Tasco Tactical scope—shown here among a few other weapons—is well suited for such occasions. This 7.62-millimeter sniper rifle is capable of sub-MOA hits. While the Stoner is not carried on most typical missions, there are times such as a regional reconnaissance where the team may be issued the weapon. This highly accurate sniper rifle may also be fitted with a sound suppressor.

Specifications:
MP5 A3
Caliber: 9-millimeter Parabellum (9x19); **weight:** (loaded with 30-round magazine) 7.53 pounds, (loaded with dual 30-round magazines) 9.08 pounds, (empty, without magazine) 6.34 pounds, empty magazine (30 rounds) .375 pounds, loaded magazine (30 rounds) 1.19 pounds; **length:** (stock extended) 25.98 inches, (stock retracted) 19.29 inches; **barrel length:** 8.85 inches; **muzzle velocity:** 1,312 fires per second; **cyclic rate:** 800 rounds per minute.

MP5 SD3
Caliber: 9-millimeter Parabellum (9x19); **weight** (loaded with 30-round magazine) 8.69 pounds, (loaded with dual 30-round magazines) 10.24 pounds, (empty, without magazine) 7.50 pounds, empty magazine (30 rounds) .375 pounds, loaded magazine (30 rounds) 1.19 pounds; **length:** (stock extended) 30.42 inches, (stock retracted) 23.97 inches; **barrel length** 5.73 inches; **muzzle velocity:** 935 fires per second; **cyclic rate:** 800 rounds per minute; **suppressor length:** 12 inches.

Colt M4
The latest pony to be released from Colt Arms of Connecticut, the M4, is a smaller, compact version of the full-sized M16A2 rifle. The design of the M4 is for the occasions when speed of action and light weight are required, as is often the case for USSOCOM forces. The barrel has been redesigned to a shortened 14.5 inches, which reduces the weight, while maintaining its effectiveness for quick-handling field operations. The retractable buttstock has intermediate stops allowing versatility in CQB without compromising shooting capabilities.

The M4 has a rifling twist of one in 7 inches, making it compatible with the full range of 5.56-millimeter ammunitions. Its sighting system contains dual apertures, allowing for 0 to 200 meters and a smaller opening for engaging targets at a longer range. Selective fire controls for the M4 have eliminated the three-round burst, replacing it with safe, semiautomatic, and full automatic fire.

The M4 has a new redesigned handguard that dissipates heat more efficiently than the previous versions of the M16 family. The redesign of the barrel also allows troops to mount the M203 grenade launcher directly onto the barrel.

The rear target sight is set up with dual apertures. The first is for a target at 0 to 200 meters and the other smaller aperture for a target at farther ranges. The rear sight is adjustable for windage and elevation.

Specifications:
Caliber: 5.56 millimeters; **weight:** (without magazine) 5.65 pounds, empty magazine (30 rounds) 2.5 pounds, loaded magazine (30 rounds) 1.0 pounds; **length:** (stock extended) 33.0 inches, (stock retracted) 29.8 inches; **barrel length:** 14.5 inches; **muzzle velocity:** (M193) 3,020 feet per second, (M855 NATO) 2,900 feet per second; **maximum effective**

In addition to the RATT and motorcycles, the STS team will often use the four-wheel-drive quad. This small 4x4 can be set up to shuttle supplies from point-to-point for the PJs. It may also be set up with an assortment of radio equipment to facilitate the ATC mission of the CCTs. By using the quad, the STT can quickly maneuver from one area of the airhead to another as the mission unfolds.

range: (M193) 393 yards, (5.56-millimeter NATO) 656 yards; **cyclic rate:** 700 to 950.

Colt M203

The M203 grenade launcher is a lightweight (3 pounds), single-shot, breech-loaded 40-millimeter weapon specifically designed for placement to the M16A1 and M16A2 rifles and M4/M16A2 carbines. The addition of the M203 to the M16 rifle or M4 carbine creates the versatility of a weapon system capable of firing both 5.56-millimeter ammunition as well as an expansive range of 40-millimeter high-explosive and special-purpose munitions.

The most commonly used ammunition is the M406 antipersonnel round. This grenade has a deadly radius of five meters. The M433 multipurpose grenade, which, in addition to the fragmentation effects, is capable of penetrating a steel armor plate up to 2 inches thick. Other types of ordnance available are buckshot, tear gas, and various signal rounds.

The receiver of the M203 is manufactured of high-strength forged aluminum alloy. This provides

Having parachuted into an airfield prior to the follow-on forces, this combat controller prepares to activate the TACAN mounted on the rear of a quad. The TACAN is an omnidirectional navigation beacon that will be used by incoming aircraft.

extreme ruggedness, while keeping weight to a minimum. A complete self-cocking firing mechanism, including striker, trigger, and positive safety lever is included in the receiver. This will allow the M203 to be operated as an independent weapon, even though attached to the M16A1, M16A2 rifles, and M4/M16A2 carbine. The barrel is also made of high-strength aluminum alloy. It slides forward in the receiver to accept a round of ammunition, then slides backward to automatically lock in the closed position, ready to fire.

Where special operation forces depend on rapid deployment, mobility, and increased firepower, where the emphasis of a small units, such as the STS, is placed on "get in and get out" fast, the addition of the M203 brings the added firepower to the already proven and outstanding family of M16 weapons.

Specifications:

Caliber: 40 millimeter; **weight:** (unloaded) 3.0 pounds, (loaded) 3.6 pounds; **length:** 15 inches, barrel length, 12 inches; **height:** (below rifle barrel center line) 3.3 inches; **width:** 3.3 inches; **velocity:** (with M406 CTG) 245 feet per second, maximum range 437 yards; **type of ammunition:** M406 high-explosive, M433 HE armor-piercing, M576 buckshot, M407 practice.

SR-25

When the situation calls for precision shooting at ground level, the STS team reaches for the Stoner SR-25. The SR-25 is a semi-automatic 7.62-millimeter rifle that can deliver rounds well out to 1,000 yards. With a 1/2-inch MOA accuracy, it has won acceptance in the special operations community as one of the finest semi-automatic sniper rifles in the world.

A product of Knight Manufacturing Company (KMC) in Florida, the SR-25 looks like an M-16 on steroids. This is no coincidence, as one of the designers of the SR-25 was Eugene Stoner, designer of the original Armalite AR-15, which later spawned the M16 family of assault rifles. The SR is derived from Stoner Rifle, and the 25 comes from adding the 10 from Eugene's AR-10 and the AR-15 series. The SR-25 makes maximum use of M16 parts, either slightly modified or unmodified. In fact, approximately 60 percent of the parts in the SR-25 are in common with the M16 family.

The logic of this design was no accident. With the M16A2 being the standard-issue weapon in the U.S. military, anyone who picks up an SR-25 immediately feels "at home." From the pistol grip to the safety switch or magazine release, if you've handled an M16/AR15 you already know how to operate the SR-25. The result of this replication is a rifle that is quicker to assimilate, easy to maintain, and more seamless in transition than any other semi-automatic 7.62-millimeter rifle in the world.

The SR-25 owes its incredible accuracy to an excellent design and demanding manufacturing by KMC. The gas system for the barrel is allowed to vibrate freely without restrictions. The 24-inch barrel is free floating so there is no interference with the barrel vibration. The handguard is a special cantilevered designed off the receiver so that any pressure on the handguard will not affect the barrel.

A member of the STT races down the tarmac still carrying his rucksack and armed with an M-4. He will search the runway for foreign objects and debris (FOD). Anything that may hamper the follow-on forces from landing will be dealt with expeditiously. If necessary the CCTs are trained to remove such obstacles with explosives.

The barrel of the SR-25 is a Remington hammer-forged blank, which is the same barrel used in the manufacture of the M24 Sniper Rifle manufactured by Remington for the U.S. Army on its M700 bolt action. The barrel features a 5R rifling and has an 11.25-to-1 twist rate. These barrels have to retain an incredible level of accuracy even after firing more than 10,000 rounds.

The upper receiver has a scope-mounting rail milled integrally into it for ease of movement and alignment of various optics. Another feature of the SR-25 is the ability to mount a sound suppresser. The muzzle blast becomes negligible, and the only sound here is the conic crack of the round going down range.

As with the M16, the SR-25 has two main sections, the upper and lower receiver. This allows for cleaning in the same manner that the troops have been familiar with since basic training. It also allows the rifle to be broken down and transported in a smaller package for clandestine activities. Once on target, the rifle is merely reassembled, with no effect on the zero of the optics.

Specifications:

Caliber: 7.62-millimeter NATO; **weight:** (without magazine and optics) 10.75 pounds, empty magazine (20 rounds), 5 pounds, loaded magazine (30 rounds) 1.16 pounds; **length:** 43.5 inches; **barrel length:** 24 inches; **muzzle velocity:** (168 g BTHP)

Whether speeding down the tarmac of a captured airfield or busting through the bush, the RATT is well designed to meet the demanding needs of the AFSOC. It can be fitted with litters to accommodate the pararescue men doing combat triage.

2,766 feet per second; **Maximum Effective Range:** (168g BTHP) 1,000 yards.

Other Equipment

It is 0300 and pitch black. Under a moonless sky a lone MC-130H passes over an enemy airstrip. There is the faint noise of a parachute being inflated, then a second and a third. Soon an STT is on the ground. They work quickly to unfasten the parachutes from their black vehicles. Running up and down the runway, these STS teams secure the runway for the follow-on troops that will soon be landing at this spot. Some of the team members are using the motorcycles to check the runway for foreign objects and debris that might get caught in an aircraft engine intake, or

perhaps pockmarks; others on four-wheel-drive quads look for obstacles that would force the aircraft to veer off course as it landed

Once the STT on the ground ensures that the runway is clear, the CCT will instruct the aircraft. Shortly after this the MC-130H touches down on an enemy airstrip. The aircraft taxies to a halt. With the props still spinning, the rear ramp opens and within moments of the cargo ramp hitting the tarmac a company of Rangers begins pouring out of the aircraft.

Pararescuemen may use the RATT to establish a triage or collection point. From this position the PJs will use the RATT to transport the wounded to awaiting aircraft as needed. The RATT is not any ordinary "jeep"; it is a four-wheel-drive tactical ambulance powered by a Porsche engine and is capable of transporting up to six litters with room for two to three PJs along to administer medical treatment. The vehicle is in its element. Whether racing down the tarmac or busting through the tree line, it is as versatile as the people behind the wheel.

While the PJs operate the RATT, other STS troops perform an foreign object debris (FOD). CCT team members are using the quads to place IR lights on the edge of the tarmac to outline the runway. Other quads are fitted with radar and radio equipment and are being set in place to provide a mobile air traffic control for the planes en route to the airfield.

GPS

How do AFSOC Pave Low pilots navigate to exact locations through the mountains? How would an STS team conduct a strategic reconnaissance, or an R&S in the dead of night traversing sand dunes and wadis in the middle of an enemy desert? A device known as Global Positioning System, or GPS.

The GPS in a collection of satellites that orbit the earth twice a day. During this orbit, they transmit the precise time, latitude, longitude, and altitude information. Using a GPS receiver, special operations forces can pinpoint their exact location anywhere on the earth.

The system was developed in the early seventies by the U.S. Department of Defense to provide a

Special Operations Forces Laser Acquisition Marker (SOFLAM): When it absolutely, positively has to be destroyed, you put an SOF team on the ground and a fast mover with a smart bomb in the air. The result: one smoking bomb crater.

The AN/PRC126 is a short-range (3- to 5-kilometer) handheld VHF tactical radio transceiver. It can be carried in a BDU pocket, or in this case a special pouch. It is widely used within the special operation forces for interteam communication.

gather these signals. The greater the number of satellites, the more dynamic the positions determine the person's location.

By measuring the time interval of the transmission and the receiving of the satellite signal, the GPS receiver calculates the distance between the users and each satellite. Using the distance measurements of at least three satellites in an algorithm computation, the GPS receiver provides the precise location. Using a special encryption signal results in Precise Positioning Service (PPS), which is used by the military. A second signal called Standard Positioning Service (SPS) is available for civilian and commercial use.

The AFSOC Special Tactics Squadrons use the Rockwell "Plugger," or PSN-11. The precise name for the unit is PLGR+96 (Precise Lightweight GPS Receiver). The PLGR96 is the most advanced version of the U.S. Department of Defense hand-held GPS units. It addresses the increasingly demanding requirements of the U.S. special operation forces.

Secure (Y-code) Differential GPS (SDGPS) allows the user to accept differential correction without zeroing the unit. Differential accuracy can be less than one meter. Other features of the Plugger include Wide Area GPS Enhancement (WAGE) for autonomous positioning accuracy to 4 meters CEP, jammer direction finding, targeting interface with laser rangefinder, remote display terminal capability, and advanced user interface features.

Weighing in at a mere 2.7 pounds (with batteries installed), the GPS unit is easily stowed in the cavernous rucksack that the STS troops carry. In addition to hand-held operation, the PLGR+96 unit can be installed into various vehicles and airborne platforms.

For missions that require the STT to travel underwater there is the Miniature Underwater Global Positioning System Receiver (MUGR). This small device weighs a mere 1.2 pounds and provides the team with position and navigational information needed for infil/exfil, fire support, SR, and target

continuous, worldwide, positioning and navigational system for U.S. military forces around the globe.

The complete constellation, as it is referred to, consists of 24 satellites orbiting approximately 12,000 miles above the earth. These 22 active and 2 reserve or back-up satellites provide data 24 hours a day for 2D and 3D positioning anywhere on the planet. Each satellite constantly broadcasts the precise time and location data. Troops using a GPS receiver

"Call for Fire." An STS team leader calls in coordinates to the AC-130U SPECTRE gunship on station using an AN/PRC-117 while his teammate provides covers with a M-4. An STT on the ground and a Spectre overhead is a lethal combination.

location. Once the unit acquires the satellite fix, the waterproof MUGR can be taken to a depth of 33 feet. Alternately, the unit may work underwater using the optional floating antenna.

SOFLAM

When it absolutely, positively has to be destroyed, you put an SOF team on the ground and a fast mover with a smart bomb in the air and the result is one smoking bomb crater. The special operations forces laser acquisition marker (SOFLAM) is is lighter and smaller than the current laser marker in service with the U.S. military. It provides the STT with the capability to locate and designate critical enemy targets for destruction using laser-guided ordnance. It can be used in daylight, or with the attached night vision optics it can be employed at night.

Radios

One of the most awesome weapons in the inventory of the Special Tactics Squadron is without a doubt

their radio. A veteran Combat Controller relates, "When the lead starts flying, the shooters think in terms of 'head to ground,' the STS team thinks in terms of 'head and above.' "

Communication is paramount in the arsenal of the STS team. You see it when they take off their floppy hats and the head gear of the PRC-126 interteam radio is visible. It is there when the team unfolds the umbrella-like satellite antennae and connects it to the compact PRC-117D. Whether using UHF, VHF, line of sight, or SATCOM, the STS teams maintain the vital link between their unit and the air assets. With this, they can call in the full weight of an AC-130U gunship circling overhead or an MH-53E Pave Low, orbiting just beyond the ridge line. As Senior Master Sergeant Philip Rhodes, AFSOC PAO, reports, "... a[n] STS team on the ground and a Spectre in the air is a lethal combination."

When the Soviet Union collapsed and the Berlin Wall came tumbling down, it marked the end to the Cold War. While the United States still has large Army divisions and vast Air Force squadrons stationed in Europe, there is not a great probability that Russian army units will be funneling through the Fulda Gap. From a soldier's view, this is good news. As good as this may seem for democracy- and freedom-loving people around the globe, it is not without its downside.

While the Soviets were aggressive and bent on world domination, they did serve a purpose. They gave us primarily one enemy to defend against, and they did keep their satellite countries in check. The end of this era left us with a dynamic world, ofttimes chaotic. Today, the U.S. military is faced with small wannabe dictators and new political gun-slingers who want to make their mark on the world.

At one time strategists ascribed to the theory that we would only fight small conflicts. Then came Desert Storm, and not since World War II had America mobilized such a vast military force. The experts figured that we would only intercede in limited bush wars, and then came Somalia and Bosnia and IFOR. There is the worldwide threat of terrorism, which has been tasted with events such as the World Trade Center bombing in the United States, the destruction of the American embassies in Tanzania and Kenya, and the list, unfortunately, goes on. Indeed, conventional forces will not be out of a job anytime in the near future. Unconventional troops, specifically special operation forces, will also continue

The scout/swimmer of an STT breaks the surface of the water and prepares to "recon" the beachhead. Once all is clear he will signal the rest of the team to come ashore, and they will begin their stealthy movement to their objective.

to be the tip of the spear as we go into the new millennium and beyond.

In all of these aforementioned incidents, the men and women of the U.S. Air Force Special Operation Command have stepped up to the task. ANYPLACE—from providing air traffic control for every allied and coalition aircraft that flew in the Persian Gulf theater of operations. ANYTIME—to the AFSOC Special Tactics Squadron sergeants who assisted in the extraction of U.S. Army Rangers in Somalia. With the current downswing of the U.S. military, it taxes the resources of all branches of the services, and Special Operations Forces are not immune. Currently one-half of the PJs who graduate from training are assigned to Air Combat Command. AFSOC gets the other half. This means that PJs are at a premium and some of the STS units are undermanned.

One of the backhanded benefits that has come from the squeeze of U.S. forces is that while one service may be overpopulated and looking to separate some of their operators, AFSOC is giving some of these shooters a home.

If you look through the ranks of a Special Tactics Squadron, it is not unusual to find a Navy SEAL or an SF-qualified staff sergeant, both now wearing the blue U.S. Air Force badges and chevrons. What is actually happening in some areas is the AFSOC STS is becoming the "Elite of the Elites."

Contrary to popular belief, only a select group of A-Teams of the Army Special Forces get to be SCUBA or HALO, or mountain-qualified. For these SF troopers, getting such training often takes months and sometimes years. For the STS teams it is not only possible to get this training, it is required to be cross-trained in all of these skills to be assigned to an AFSOC unit.

It is not unusual to find an SF-qualified trooper in a Special Tactics Squadron. This staff sergeant transferred from the Army to AFSOC. A former U.S. Army Special Forces medical sergeant, Staff Sergeant Gregg Fox now operates on an STT as a pararescueman, or PJ. Having passed all SF qualifications, he is authorized to wear the "Special Forces" tab.

As AFSOC enters the next millennium, the members of the Special Tactics Squadrons will continue to be the tip of the spear in U.S. special operations forces. They will, more often than not, be on site before any other forces. They will often serve as the eyes and ears of USSOCOM, and if necessary they will bring in the muscle of the air assets of AFSOC, living up to their mottoes, "First There," "That Others May Live."

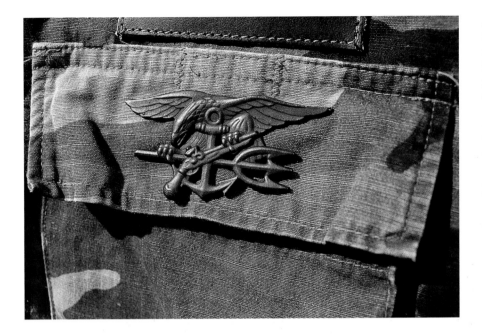

As with the occasional SF tab, as you look through the ranks of the Air Force's Special Tactics Squadrons you may also notice the sporadic trident of the U.S. Navy SEALs. With the downsizing of U.S. military forces, members of other elite units are finding new homes in the Special Tactic Squadrons. These combat-tested veterans bring additional battlefield expertise to the Air Commando heritage.

When you have to hump a ruck with the SF ODA or lock-out of a sub with the SEALs, you have to be able to keep pace with the other shooters, or you are a liability to the mission and the men. If this happens, you can be certain that they will not request your services again. If, and it is the case with STS, you can keep up with the Green Berets and the "Men with Green Faces," then you are a valuable asset to any unit. Any commanders worth their salt will move heaven and earth to get you assigned to their theater of operations.

As AFSOC goes into the twenty-first century, the STS team will see the incorporation of high-tech equipment. Today there is the air traffic control simulator that can show the CCT the view of numerous airports and airfields, viewed in a variety of weather conditions in night or daylight environments. When he hits the ground, he'll already be familiar with the lay of the land. Further research is being done with special helmets that are linked to computers and satellites. These units will provide the wearer with tactical information via a heads-up display or HUD unit in the visor. Combat controllers will be able to see navigational data on the visor, while the PJ may bring up a procedure from a medical library contained in a computer in their rucksack. Holographic devices, improved night vision goggles (NVG), and thermal imagers may be found in the rucksacks of the STT in the not-so-distant future.

The aircrews above and the STS teams on the ground will continue to excel at that which they do best. The crew of an MC-130H will penetrate enemy air defenses to deliver an SOF team. A Combat Shadow will refuel a CV-22 somewhere over, oops—sorry, that's classified. Days before an assault, an STT will perform a Regional Survey of an HLZ; and a Pave Low will fly in under enemy radar, skimming above the terrain below, to perform a CSAR.

These are the Quiet Professionals of the U.S. Air Force Special Operations Command.

The Air Commandos of the twenty-first century who carry on the tradition—ANYTIME, ANYPLACE.

AT: Antiterrorism. Defensive measures used to reduce the vulnerability of individuals and property to terrorism.

C4I: Command, control, communications, computers, and intelligence.

CinC: Commander in chief.

Civil affairs: The activities of a commander that establish, maintain, influence, or exploit relations between military forces and civil authorities, both governmental and nongovernmental, and the civilian population in a friendly, neutral, or hostile area of operations to facilitate military operations and consolidate operational objectives. Civil affairs may include performance by military forces of activities and functions normally the responsibility of the local government. These activities may occur prior to, during, or subsequent to military action. They may also occur, if directed, in the absence of other military operations.

Clandestine operation: Activities sponsored or conducted by governmental departments or agencies in such a way as to ensure secrecy or concealment. (It differs from covert operations in that emphasis is placed on concealment of the operation rather than on concealment of the identity of the sponsor.) In Special Operations, an activity may be both covert and clandestine and may focus equally on operational considerations and intelligence-related activities.

Close air support (CAS): Air action against hostile targets that are in close proximity to friendly forces and require detailed integration of each air mission with the fire and movement of those forces.

Collateral special operations activities: Collateral activities in which special operations forces, by virtue of their inherent capabilities, selectively may be tasked to participate. These include security assistance, humanitarian assistance, antiterrorism, and other security activities, counterdrug operations, personnel recovery, and special activities.

Counterproliferation: Activities taken to counter the spread of dangerous military capabilities, and allied technologies or know-how, especially weapons of mass destruction and ballistic missile delivery systems.

Counterterrorism: Offensive measures taken to prevent, deter, and respond to terrorism.

Covert operations: Operations planned and executed to conceal the identity of or permit plausible denial by the sponsor.

Crisis: An incident or situation involving a threat to the United States, its territories, citizens, military forces and possessions, or vital interests that develops rapidly and creates a condition of such diplomatic, economic, political, or military importance that commitment of U.S. military forces and resources is contemplated to achieve national objectives.

Direct action mission: In special operations, a specified act involving operations of an overt, covert, clandestine, or low-visibility nature conducted primarily by a sponsoring power's special operations forces in hostile or denied areas.

Ducks: Types of Zodiac deployments.
  Double: Twin Zodiacs.
  Hard: Zodiac with hard metal bottom.
  Soft: Zodiac raft.
  K: Kangaroo.
  T: Tethered.

Exfiltration: The removal of personnel or units from areas under enemy control.

First line belt: Specially designed webbing with a shock cord inside, used when traveling on aircraft. One end has a standard carabiner and the other end has a quick-release carabiner.

Foreign internal defense: Participation by civilian and military agencies of a government in any action programs taken by another government to free and protect its society from subversion, lawlessness, and insurgency.

Guerrilla warfare: Military and paramilitary operations conducted in enemy-held or hostile territory by irregular, predominantly indigenous forces.

Host nation: A nation that receives the forces or supplies of allied nations or NATO organizations to be located on, operate in, or transit through its territory.

Humanitarian assistance: Assistance provided by Department of Defense forces, as directed by appropriate authority, in the aftermath of natural or manmade disasters to help reduce conditions that present a serious threat to life and property. Assistance provided by United States forces is limited in scope and duration and is designed to supplement efforts of civilian authorities that have primary responsibility for providing such assistance.

Infiltration: The movement through or into an area or territory occupied by either friendly or enemy troops or organizations. The movement is made, either by small groups or by individuals, at extended or irregular intervals. When used in connection with the enemy, it implies that contact is avoided.

Insurgency: An organized movement aimed at the overthrow of a constituted government through the use of subversion and armed conflict.

Internal defense: The full range of measures taken by a government to free and protect its society from subversion, lawlessness, and insurgency.

Interoperability: The ability of systems, units, or forces to provide services to and to accept services from other systems, units or forces, or use the services so exchanged to enable them to operate effectively together.

Low-intensity conflict: Political-military confrontation between contending states or groups below conventional war and above routine, peaceful competition among states. It frequently involves protracted struggles of competing principles and ideologies. Low-intensity conflict ranges from subversion to the use of armed force. It is waged by a combination of means employing political, economic, informational, and military instruments. Low-intensity conflicts are often localized, generally in the Third World, but contain regional and global security implications.

METT-T: Mission, Enemy, Troops, Terrain, and Time. Perimeters that affect the mission profile of the AFSOC task, including STS CSAR or Spectre CAS. These five criteria must be addressed in the mission planning.

Military civic action: The use of indigenous military forces on projects useful to the local population at all levels in such fields as education, training, public works, agriculture, transportation, communications, health, sanitation, and others contributing to economic and social development.

Mission: A statement of our reason for being and what we wish to accomplish an an organization

Nation assistance: Civil or military assistance rendered to a nation's territory during peacetime, crises, or emergencies, or war based on agreements mutually concluded between nations. Nation assistance programs include, but are not limited to, security assistance, FID, other Department of Defense (DOD) Title 10 programs, and activities performed on a reimbursable basis by federal agencies or international organizations.

NCA: National Command Authorities. The president and the secretary of defense together or their duly deputized alternates or successors. The term signifies constitutional authority to direct the Armed Forces in their execution of military action.

Objectives: Specific actions to be achieved in a specified time period. Accomplishment will indicate progress toward achieving the goals.

Operator: See "Shooter."

Psychological operations: Planned operations to convey selected information and indicators to foreign audiences to influence their emotions, motives, objective reasoning, and ultimately the behavior of foreign government, organizations, groups, and individuals. The purpose of psychological operations is to induce or reinforce foreign attitudes and behavior favorable to the originator's objectives.

Ranger assist cord: A 550 cord (parachute line) used to attach anything and everything to an operator.

RAMZ: Rigging Alternate Method Zodiac (pronounced rams). Procedure for air-dropping a Zodiac raft.

REDS: Rapid Extrication Deployment System, similar to the "jaws of life."

Rubber NUGS: Training weapons manufactured of rubber and metal to military specifications.

Shooter: Special operations forces trooper: U.S. Army Special Forces, U.S. Navy SEAL, U.S. Army Ranger, SAS (British or Australian), and so on.

Special reconnaissance: Reconnaissance and surveillance actions conducted by special operations forces to obtain or verify, by visual observation or other collection methods, information concerning the capabilities, intentions, and activities of an actual or potential enemy or to secure data concerning the meteorological, hydrographic, or geographic characteristics of a particular area. It includes target acquisition, area assessment, and post-strike reconnaissance.

Strategy: Methods, approaches, or specific moves taken to implement and attain an objective.

Unconventional warfare: A broad spectrum of military and paramilitary operations conducted in enemy-held, enemy-controlled, or politically sensitive territory. Unconventional warfare includes, but is not limited to, the interrelated fields of guerrilla warfare, evasion and escape, subversion, sabotage, and other operations of a low-visibility, covert, or clandestine nature. These interrelated aspects of unconventional warfare may be prosecuted singularly or collectively by predominantly indigenous personnel, usually supported and directed in varying degrees by (an) external source(s) during all conditions of war or peace.

Abbreviations

AFSOC	Air Force Special Operations Command
AFSOF	Air Force Special Operations facility
ARSOC	Army Special Operations Command
CAP	Combat Air Patrol
CAS	Close air support
CIA	Central Intelligence Agency
CCT	Combat control team
CRRC	Combat rubber raiding craft
CSAR	Combat search and rescue
CT	Counterterrorism
CQB	Close quarters battle
DA	Direct action
DOD	Department of Defense
DZ	Drop zone
E&E	Evasion and escape
EW	Electronic warfare
FAC	Forward air control
FARRP	Forward area refueling and re-arming point
FID	Foreign internal defense
FLIR	Forward looking infrared
FOB	Forward operation base
FOD	Foreign object/debris
FRIS	Fast rope insertion system
GPS	Global positioning system
HAHO	High altitude high opening
HALO	High altitude low opening
HE	High explosive
HEI	High explosive incendiary
HUMINT	Human intelligence
IFAM	Initial familiarization
IIN	Integrated inertial navigation
INTREP	Intelligence report
JCS	Joint Chiefs of Staff
JTF	Joint Task Force
LBE	Load bearing equipment
LZ	Landing zone
MRE	Meal ready to eat
MTT	Mobile training team
NOE	Nape of the Earth
NOD	Night optical device
NVG	Night vision goggles
PJ	Pararescue jumper
PSYWAR	Psychological warfare
RAMZ	Rigid alternate method Zodiac
REDS	Rapid Extrication Deployment System
RST	Reconnaissance and surveillance team
SEAL	Sea Air Land (U.S. Navy Special Forces)
SAR	Search and rescue
SAS	Special Air Service
SF	Special Forces (U.S. Army)
SOCOM	Special Operation Command
SOF	Special Operations Forces
SOFLAM	Special operations forces laser acquisition marker
SPIES	Special procedure insertion extraction system
SR	Special reconnaissance
SST	SAR security team
STT	Special tactics teams
USASOC	U.S. Army Special Operations Command
UW	Unconventional warfare

Index